I AM THE QUEEN BEE

How I Overcame Self-Sabotage To Fly Anyway and How You Can Too.

DANI WALLACE

CONTENTS

DEDICATION

For my Gram, Rene Lyon.

The OG Queen Bee, who taught me the importance of telling stories. I wish you could see us now.

For my Mum, Irene, for being a warrior queen and for raising warrior queens. Your strength has been our strength, even when you don't realise it.

For my sister Gems, we know better, so we do better. We are the cycle breakers.

For my Flowers and The Reds, the next generation of Queen Bees...The world is yours.

People like us can. People like us do.

Go get 'em, my darlings.

FOREWORD

Being unapologetically you.

Sounds simple, doesn't it?

But in a world where seemingly, we are rewarded for fitting in, feeling like you are the 'odd one out' most of the time and being knocked down and boxed off when you dare to be different can make you want to give up.

I implore you.

Don't.

Let me tell you a brief story; some years ago I wrote a book - I never expected it to be a thing, being honest, I never expected to be a 'thing' myself

But here I am, and I have changed literally hundreds of thousands of lives.

It's insane.

I dared to dream.

I dared to be different.

I dared to do.

Which leads me on to Dani.....

Now Dani is the embodiment of the philosophies that I hold so dear such as doing the work, standing out, giving back AND doing it all without sacrificing who you are and what you believe in.

This book, if you apply those lessons, in time - will change your life.

You just have to believe in yourself and believe that you are worthy, much like I believe in Dani.

I truly wish you the best on your journey; I can't promise you *when* you will get there but if you keep going all while being - yes - unapologetically you (it does take a little bit of practice) you *will* get there.

Take the lessons Dani teaches you, apply them daily, and see your life change for the better.

Good luck.

Dan Meredith

Author of best-selling book - How To Be F*kcing Awesome

Entrepreneur at www.coffeewithdan.com

ABOUT THE AUTHOR

Dani Wallace is a motivational speaker, international celebrity public speaking coach and fearless leader of the I Am The Queen Bee Movement. She helps people the world over Show Up, Wise Up and Rise Up so that they can take life by the big ol' lady balls and step up into their birthright of success.

Dani is an entrepreneurial mum of three who has overcome homelessness, domestic violence and years of self-sabotage. She has gone on to run sell-out live events, a global online community, and helps entrepreneurs, celebrities and businesses speak the world over.

Her message that, even though it is important that we acknowledge our adversities, it is *vital* that we pay forward our strengths has seen the I Am The Queen Bee Movement gather momentum and it shows no signs of slowing.

Dani, a former senior leadership trainer in the corporate space for over a decade and a singer and entertainer for over 20 years, is on a mission to spread the word that, whatever your background, whatever troubles you have faced, whatever level you are at, Bees don't care what humans think is impossible, they FLY ANYWAY.

facebook.com/thequeenbeedani

twitter.com/thequeenbeedani

instagram.com/thequeenbeedani

linkedin.com/in/thequeenbeedani

youtube.com/thequeenbeedani

INTRODUCTION

You may or may not have read my first book, a little 'How To' book about how to get speaking – Closed Mouths Don't Get Fed. (That's right, I'ma go ahead and start with a shameless plug.)

In Chapter One of it, I talk about Imposter Syndrome. More specifically, I speak about my own imposter syndrome and what it sounds like.

Mine sounds like the fabulous Nikki Grahame from 2006's Big Brother.

Whenever I attempt something that I know is going to have me level up or is going to reach more people than I have done previously, she rears her head, vehemently calling me out. She rocks up in my mind's eye, full tantrum, wild-eyed, yelling as loud as she can, 'Who IS she?!!? Who IS this person thinking she can roll up and share her shit like it's going to magically help someone?!?!?'

It's really quite distracting, especially as I sit here at 12.30 pm on a Sunday in August, having just waved my husband and kids off for a few days away while I write this book.

I have to take a second and take a breath. See, this book has been burning inside me for a few years now. It has been on my mind for the longest time that if I can help just one person to choose to fly anyway, regardless of where they come from or what they have previously thought they were capable of, I'll be happy.

I wanted to create something for all of you out there who have felt this.

You may be feeling scared about taking the plunge and making a significant life change.

You may want to start your own business.

You may wish to leave a job you have felt stuck in for a long time.

You may wish to take back control of your shit after giving away your power to someone or something, and it's time for you to rise up.

Whatever it is, me listening to this inner tantrum is helping neither of us.

One of the main themes we will cover in this book is how I came to grips with the things that were previously holding me back, how I made them my bitch and then how I went on to turn the knowledge I gained during the battle into a superpower. Into a survival guide for those that come across me.

I'm a speaker and speaker coach by trade these days and I have written this book like a series of talks. Short topics, stories and learnings that, when you squish 'em all together, form a veritable arsenal of awesome.

If you like, you can go ahead and read this book from cover to cover. Hopefully, I have managed to get all the subjects into an order that will allow for this and for it all to make sense.

Alternatively, you can dip into this book at whichever chapter tickles your pickle and glean what you need that way.

Either way rocks.

In the first part of the book, I will share with you the experiences I had that brought me to create the IATQB Movement.

In the second part of the book, I will share with you the things that I learned and implemented that saw me create the success and abundance that I am blessed with today.

Like everything that I do, there are no hard and fast rules here.

And this is where I want to begin our journey.

If we are all to start stepping into being our own version of Queenliness, or Kingliness, or Royalness (all are welcome, encouraged and loved here), then we have to get comfortable with the fact that, just like everything else in business and life, it is within us to create our own rules,[1] even if you start with how you read a book.

So, let's dive in.

Let us begin our royal quest together.

And when the internal Nikki[2] rears her head while I'm writing this (and she will, it happens to the best of us) asking me the dreaded question...

'Who IS she?!'

I will breathe, lean in and answer, as I have done throughout this journey of self-discovery...

'I am Dani Fucking Wallace, and I Am The Queen Bee.'

_____

1. Please keep within the realms of the law of your particular land – I'm ok for lawsuits, ta.

2. I'm absolutely positive that Nikki Grahame is a glorious human being and I would love to give her a big cuddle in real life to apologise for what my subconscious has created in her image.

WE'RE GONNA BE FRIENDS

Hey friend! (That's what we are now, btw. We're gonna spend a fair chunk of time together and I don't spend my time with just anyone, y' know.)

Welcome to the world of IATQB! I would say make yourself comfortable, but I wouldn't be doing my job at all correctly if that's how we kick off proceedings.

Some of the things we are going to cover in this book are designed to make you feel a little, maybe sometimes even a lot, uncomfortable.

Being a good friend means sometimes you have to call each other out on your shit. I will endeavour to do this in as loving a way as possible.

Your comfort has kept you where you are for so long, and you would not be reading this book if that is where you wanted to stay.

Comfort, while lovely for a time, is not where we are, as members of the mammalian family, designed to reside.

Think about it. Reaaalllyyy think about this...

I have a gift for you. Tomorrow, you can have a lie-in. Go ahead; you can get up whenever the heck you like.

Lord KNOWS we need a lie-in, right?

You need a rest... so rest. Then, when you have rested, you can just go ahead and stay in bed—all snuggly under that duvet. I'll have someone bring up the snacks.

In fact, turn Netflix on. You have my explicit permission to binge-watch a whole series of whatever takes your fancy.

Stay the eff in bed. Rest some more. Even into the next day if you like.

But here's the thing: once the Netflix series and snacks have run out, maybe even before, you're going to notice that you're aching. You will feel actual physical pain, even though you are supposed to be 'comfortable'.

Your body and your mind are not designed to be 'comfortable' for extended periods of time.

The pleasure we take within it is designed so that we rest, but if we stay there, there are dire consequences.

This is why relationships fail, friendships falter, businesses stagnate. We get comfortable, and we stop working on them.

You can be comfortable and then wake up and be into your old age and never have felt anything else except lethargy and apathy.

This is not the life for which you are designed. You are not stepping into your fucking BIRTHRIGHT of success, abundance, peace, great relationships and more, if comfort is where you wish to reside.

You will feel comfort and all of the aching that goes with it and then what?

You die.

Ooooft.

I found myself in this position when I was working in the corporate world. I had found a job that allowed me to be comfortable. It also allowed the people closest to me to feel satisfied that I was 'safe'.

It was a 'proper job'.

Previously, I had been singing all over the world. I had contracts performing and compering from Lanzarote to the

USA and all kinds of place in between but still, because they didn't see what it was that I was doing day in, day out, my family and friends really wanted me to come home and lay down some roots.

Because that's the done thing, isn't it?

Go to school. Go to college. Go to university. Get a proper job. Get married. Buy a house. Have babies. Retire. Die.

Ergh.

It wasn't how I wanted my life to go down.

I felt it within me, even from a young age when I decided that there was only so much writing about performance I wanted to do so dropped out of college, that I was not destined for this path.

Don't get me wrong; this is not about delusions of grandeur. I truly wanted to make a difference in the world. I heard a quote when I was younger that always stuck with me.

66 **"To leave the world a bit better, whether by a healthy child, a garden patch, or a redeemed social condition; to know that even one life has breathed easier because you have lived - that is to have succeeded."**

— RALPH WALDO EMERSON.

To leave the world a better place than when you found it was a concept that I could get down with, but I had no idea how, so I plodded on.

The pull of the comfort of my family and friends meant I came back to the UK and took a job, and as with most things I turn my hand to, because I'm a tenacious and stubborn little mare, I did ok.

I worked my way up the corporate ladder landing some really cool roles, mostly within the learning and development space, eventually moving into management because that was the correct path, right?

But here's the thing. I didn't give a shit about the job. After a while in the corporate sector, I started to see through what it had me doing.

I was doing as little as possible to earn as much as possible without getting found out. I was seeking comfort, and it was making me ache.

It was the ultimate honey trap. (NOW we get to the bee-related analogies. I'm surprised it took me so long to be honest.)

I was working 50 - 60 hours a week, lining someone else's pocket and managing people who did not want to be managed because, for the most part, they were in the same honey trap.

I learned to teach, and I learned to lead, BUT the people I was working with did not want to be led. They were all 'comfortable' too.

So, I gave up. I stopped showing up within the role because I didn't want to manage.

To manage means to 'get by' and that's all I was doing, and it wasn't enough. Sure, I turned up every day, but my apathy was palpable. I was desperately unhappy in my work, and no one was benefitting.

It also told in the way that my team and superiors responded to me. They would be disrespectful, regardless of how nice I was. They would backbite and gossip. They would blame me for things that weren't my fault because I was an easy scapegoat, seeing as I was letting the ball drop in so many other areas.

It truly was a shit show and all for the sake of 'comfort'.

I'd got to the point where I was crying in my kitchen because I was sad that the only place I sang any more was there. It felt pathetic really, but apart from the children, my life felt joyless.

My cup was not being filled up, and I could see myself frittering away my life before my very eyes, and it scared the hell out of me.

Who was I giving back to?

What was the purpose of all this?

How in the world was I going to leave the world a better place than I found it if this was all I was going to do?

So, when I inevitably got sacked for essentially not giving a shit, I decided it was big girl pants time, and I'd best put some thought into what the fuck I actually wanted to do with my life.

I was waiting for a sign, and here it was.

With my safe paycheck taken away from me, I needed to make sure I moved my now very uncomfortable ass pretty quickly to keep my head above water.

It was the best thing that ever happened to me.

Comfort is a trap. It is designed to help you enjoy your rest time, but if it's rest for the rest of your life you're after, you're in the wrong place. You are short serving your entire existence.

Get up!

Move!

Let's get gloriously uncomfortable.

We have shit to do, and it won't get done without you.

It is not my intention to spark existential crisis within you, but you have to remember, my darling new friend, that you are reading this book because you want more for yourself and we are not here for a long time in the grand scheme of things, so we'd best get cracking.

I want more for you too. That's why I'm here. I'm ready to cheerlead you through all your discomfort. I even brought pom-poms. That's what friends do, right?

BECOMING THE QUEEN BEE

WHEN I MAKE the statement 'I Am The Queen Bee', I am aware that it is pretty audacious. It is a bold statement when you rock up in places declaring yourself royalty, yet that is precisely what I do.

Let's get clear on what making this statement actually means.

I have no designs on over-throwing our monarchy. I'm a fan, in fact.

Such a fan am I that it properly boiled my piss when I realised that I had not been born into it and I had, in fact, been born to a working-class family on the council estates of Preston.

I love our royal family, particularly Great Britain's very own Queen Bee, our wonderful Queen Elizabeth II, and how she has served our country as long as she has.

I just find it wholly unfair that my family struggled to make ends meet, and there were people out there that were born into riches.

Once the shit show of my early adult life was over, I started to reclaim some of the power that I had relinquished for many years. I began to switch from thinking that success, wealth, happiness and all the good stuff were not for me, to believing that I just had to be a bit more creative about making them happen.

They were still my birthright.

Just like the Queen.

And it is not just MY birthright: it is YOURS too.

(The whole bee thing, I will cover in chapter 4.)

Of all the stories I will share with you in this book, this is the one that, most likely, you will have heard/read about if you have come across me before.

I mean, it's a lot to unpack, this life of mine. So far, it has been quite a ride. I'm going to try and condense the key bits of my formative years into just a chapter as the real magic started to happen after this.

Actually, this chapter will cover the first 30 years of my life while the rest will take care of the other six. (At the time of writing this book I am a youthful 36 years old.) We may jump around the timeline a bit, but I did warn you that this book wasn't going to conform to regular book writing or storytelling rules. We make our own rules, see?

The first 30 years of my life, I flapped about in the dark, holding on to what I thought I 'should' do, playing out lots of learned behaviours (see Chapter 5), and I did not fare well.

We did not have a lot growing up. We were of an era and in an area where there was lots of month left at the end of the money.

Hand-me downs were sometimes fifth or sixth hand by the time they got to yours truly.

There was a running joke that when the ice-cream van came around blaring its tinny nursery rhyme siren, it meant that they had run out of ice-cream so that we didn't ask for one.

The Friday 'Big Shop' was done frugally, with a calculator and coupons and it was a total win if we could get to the supermarket at the same time that they were reducing the

price of short-dated fresh produce. Shopping for 'Whoop-
sies' was definitely a thing.

Holidaying was cheap and cheerful when we were able.
We would go to caravan sites on the coast with a suitcase
full of food for the week. I have fond memories of the entertainment at these parks. In the daytime, there would be fun
kids' clubs, and in the evening, we would get into the entertainment lounge early to bag a good table ready for the
bingo, kids' disco and evening show.

There were talent shows that formed part of the evening
entertainment, and we would have me enter knowing I was
pretty much guaranteed to win and therefore get an extra
few days' holiday for the prestigious 'Park Finals' come
October time.

We had two holidays a year but not in the flash way most
people did. I knew how to be tenacious and make stuff
happen, even as a kid.

Dad was an alcoholic. A functioning alcoholic but one
nevertheless. He was tormented by demons that he couldn't
face when sober, so when night fell and the cans of
cider/strong lager opened, they reared their heads and my
mum, and later on my sister and I, bore the brunt of his
dissatisfaction and inadequacies.

There was a duality in our family. On the one hand, there
was a lot of love. Love by the boatload. Our family was an

anchor for our cousins. It was like our house had a revolving door for all of them at some point to live with us while my aunties and uncles had struggles of their own. My mum would take them in, help build them back up and send them back out into the world.

Mum, even now, is one of life's incredible caregivers. She was forced to finish school at fifteen to look after her grandmother, who had dementia, while her mum, my grandma, would work in the family business to keep a roof over their heads.

Looking after and loving people is what my Mum does best. I have yet to meet someone who cares so fiercely about folk. She taught my sister and me a capacity for love, affection and honesty, paired with a zero-tolerance for bullshit. My Mumma is a force to be reckoned with, so it was a surprise to many the things that she dealt with behind closed doors.

I remember summers and Christmases with sometimes up to six kids bunking up in one bedroom. They became our brothers and sisters, and we grew up with the intense and shared knowledge of our families and their misgivings in a way that only siblings could. They were our playmates and fellow survivors of the storms that ravaged our parents' lives.

On the other hand, Dad struggled with the constant comings and goings as he was battling his own issues, and the emotional and psychological abuse of my mum began. To all of which, my sister and I bore witness.

Unpacking the events of these years isn't helpful to you or to me. When I decided to write about this part of my life, I wanted to avoid graphic detail because this is not the aim of this book. Also, my dad isn't in a position to defend himself. Suffice to say we experienced every nuance and facet of domestic abuse during this time, from the insidious gaslighting to out and out violence.

As it does for many who experience domestic abuse in their later years, it was the exposure to this kind of behaviour that went on to inform a lot of the choices I made in my relationships when I grew up. (Although, let's use the term 'grown-up' super loosely.)

When I was about eight, my primary school teacher, Elaine Sutton, got in touch with my mum and suggested that I have singing lessons. Mum, unable at the time to afford more formal tutoring, paid Elaine a couple of pounds a week to teach me the basics of music and singing.

It was in singing and performing that I found a way to channel my energies.

Our house was a busy one, what with people coming and going all the time, and being the youngest and also a natural extrovert, it was difficult to be seen and heard by anyone.

Despite being naturally very intelligent, no one took much notice of me unless I sang.

So, sing, I did. In fact, singing and travel were the only things I could see myself doing with my life.

The desire to travel, looking back, was primarily due to the fact I wanted to run away from where I was. I wanted to be as far away as possible from where and how I grew up.

This put me in quite the conundrum because, in order to travel, I would need to have money: flights don't pay for themselves, right? So, I figured, if I couldn't *pay* to travel, I would need to *be paid* to travel! (I was a tenacious little bugger, remember?!)

Revelling in my own genius, I set about auditioning for all sorts of performer jobs across the world.

It was an incredible experience; it truly was. Equally, it was hard work for pretty low pay, but still, one month I would be waking up with beautiful Argassi village and Ionian Sea views and the next I would be lying under a starry sky in Finland gazing at the Northern Lights.

From Lanzarote to the USA, I sang and danced my way around the world, performing solo shows and big stage productions. It was glorious. All the time I was away, I didn't have to think about home.

After a few years of this, I felt that pull from my family and friends that I spoke to you about earlier. Part of this pull was that my lovely Grandma, Rene, was nearing the end of her time on this earthly plane and I wanted to be close to her.

So, with my then boyfriend, I moved back to Preston to pursue a 'proper job'. One more befitting someone entering their mid-20s.

I got myself said job, we bought a house, had a baby (my gorgeously quirky and beautiful Poppy Grace) and sent out invites to our wedding. Because that's what you do, right?

Buying the house was a massive deal for me. It was something that was seemingly unobtainable for such a long time. It was a symbol of the roots that I secretly really wanted to put down after years of running away. I had never really owned anything of value before, and this was mine.

Job, house, kids, marriage... these were all things that were expected of me at this point and, in coming back to the UK, I had set myself on a path of settling. Of comfort. The kind of comfort that makes you ache.

This comfort was short-lived as very soon after sending the invites out to our wedding, my then fiancé realised that he was not ready for all the trappings of growing up and, quite abruptly, left.

I don't blame him for leaving; I had practically railroaded the poor guy into fitting into my cookie-cutter life. He did both of us a favour.

We weren't a particularly good fit. I was ambitious and driven while he was super laid back with no real wish to achieve much. Had we wed, it probably wouldn't have lasted too long anyway, and, to this day, I wish him well.

Nevertheless, at the time my world was rocked, as you can imagine, and I was left feeling particularly vulnerable.

I had been thrown into first-time parenting and single-parenthood in one fell swoop when I thought I had set up my whole life so well.

Getting to grips with juggling my career and my beautiful new baby was proving both difficult and draining. My mental health was taking a nose-dive, and I started to slip into depression and self-loathing.

It was all I could do, most days, to keep the two of us alive and fed even though, to the world, I was holding things together. My life was a shambles, yet people would comment on how strong I was, and this made me laugh. Strong was a million miles away from how I was truly feeling.

It was within this vulnerability that I met the father of my second daughter. I considered him handsome and exciting if a little dangerous. A world away from my previous partner. He showered me with the affection that my wounded ego and heart craved.

The first month of our relationship was a heady mix of the attention and romance I sought and found lacking in my previous relationships, but he also brought a huge wave of relief.

Being a single parent is relentless. The sleepless nights, feeding, and everything else that goes with parenting when there is no-one to share the load is HARD. You can imagine my delight when this guy showed up like some knight in shining armour. He would decorate the house, put rose petals in my bath, let me go for naps when I was exhausted and cooked for me when I couldn't bring myself to. This all sounds lovely, but it was a lot, and it happened very quickly.

In domestic abuse or narcissistic terms, this is known as 'love-bombing'- the act of storming the gates of resistance or protection with flattery and acts of extreme kindness to gain favour and eventually control, which is precisely what happened.

Very quickly, we got into a relationship and almost as quickly, as with most situations like this where vulnerable women meet their narcissistic abuser, this relationship turned sour.

I had ended up exactly where I had been trying to escape from my whole life — in a violent and abusive relationship. We were like horrific magnets toward each other.

As with the stories I could tell you about my experiences with dad, I won't delve into the ins and outs of the horror of these short but painful years, but it was a textbook situation.

For anyone who may think that they could be experiencing domestic abuse, I will put links at the back of the book to help you; the National Domestic Violence Helpline was an absolute God-send when I needed it.

It was a roller coaster couple of years which culminated in several police interventions and an injunction that was granted by the courts to put the distance necessary between us.

This relationship did have a beautiful silver lining in the form of the ray of sunshine that is my second daughter, Daisy Faith, and I would go through it all again to have her. She smiled from being the tiniest dot. She was a light in the darkest of times, and between her and my darling Poppy, I had two precious reasons to pull through.

My daughters' middle names are all virtues I needed to be reminded of at the time, and Faith, at this point, was definitely required.

Soon after this, because of the financial struggle to keep both my girls in nursery in order to keep some semblance of routine and stability in their lives, paired with the shame that would come from quitting work, I lost my house.

I mean, it didn't just disappear into thin air, that would be both ludicrous and miraculous. I just couldn't afford to keep up the repayments on the mortgage.

The house that had been, besides my beautiful children, the first 'real' thing I had achieved, had been snatched away from me. It solidified in my mind at the time that people like me were not destined for good or nice things. I was heartbroken and ashamed.

We became homeless, and it was a bitter pill to swallow. Our family and friends rallied and allowed us to sofa surf with them, but the shame filled me like a poison.

It was in this space that I constructed a litany of misdemeanours in my mind that exemplified why it would make more sense if I just weren't around any more.

Despite my best efforts, I was a failure.

I wasn't respected in my work.

I believed that I couldn't make a good decision to save my life.

I was a burden to all those around me, particularly my family and my kids.

My friends had all but given up on me because I had pushed them away.

I was failing at everything and only holding onto my job by the skin of my teeth.

I was utterly unlovable.

I struggled to show up for myself, let alone for anyone else.

All of these were huge untruths, of course, but I was in such a poor mental state that I couldn't see the good in anything about myself.

One night, I was tucking my girls into bed at my mum's as I was about to leave for work in London. I didn't know if I was kissing them goodbye, or goodnight.

I sat in the car that night and cried.

I wanted the pain to stop.

I wanted to end it, but I didn't know how.

How could I stop feeling such shame every time I looked at my girls?

What kind of mum was I anyway?

What kind of daughter/sister/friend was I to anyone?

In this cataclysmic wave of pain and anguish, once I had cried till my throat was sore, and my eyes were swollen, I was left with one thought.

Either life was going to keep happening to me, or I'd better start happening to life.

How the fuck was I going to leave the world in a better place than I found it if I jumped ship now?

Surely it would be worse? My poor girls would be left thinking my departure was their fault, and I already knew what carrying the burdens of your parents felt like and fuck doing that to them.

So, I made a choice.

It was time I stopped pissing and moaning, and actually did the things I needed to do to get myself into a position of strength.

I chose to take back control.

I threw myself into building myself back up. I consumed personal development books like they were going out of fashion, and I set to work on trying to like myself and, eventually, love myself again.

It was a hard slog, clawing my way back from the brink but I swore to myself that I would never allow myself to feel that desolate and desperate again.

The power was mine to take back and take it back I did.

The things that I learned about and applied to myself during this time are the things that I will share with you in the coming pages of this book.

A couple of years later, I was sitting on the sofa, with my girls, in a house we had managed to find soon after the moment I just described.

I had met my now husband, Mark, had my third and final daughter, Ivy Hope (it was nice to have some foliage to finish off my bouquet), and I was working for myself, finally doing the things I loved.

We were watching The Bee Movie (2007), and there was this quote at the start that floored me:

> **"According to all known laws of aviation, there is no way a bee should be able to fly. Its wings are too small to get its fat little body off the ground. The bee, of course, flies anyway, because bees don't care what humans think is impossible."**

The realisation hit me like a bolt of lightning. I finally knew my purpose.

In my mind, I went back to my mum's house that awful night when I felt like ending it all and I remembered how I made a choice.

I chose to fly anyway.

When I decided to choose life, I also decided to make it my mission to help anyone that I was able to realise that they could choose to fly too.

Since then, telling this story, and in turn, helping others tell their own stories, has become my mission.

Our stories are powerful and have the potential to become another person's survival guide.

AWESOME THINGS THAT BEES DO

So we have now firmly established the Queenly part of I Am The Queen Bee... what of the bee bit?

Bees really do rock my world for soooo many reasons.

Everything about bees makes me happy. The historical and scientific way in which they are revered is sound proof that I am definitely not alone.

From Manchester, England, adopting the worker bee as a symbol of its vibrant industrial history, to the Druids honouring bees with the symbolism of community, celebration and abundance, the humble bee means a lot to many.

Bees do incredible things that we can, certainly in business, draw great analogies and learning from. I rely on our fuzzy-bottomed friends for that very thing, particularly when I speak about the importance of community.

Let me share some of their awesome little quirks with you.

The Waggle Dance

Probably one of the more well-known of bee behaviours, the waggle dance is among one of my favourites.

Scarcity in business communities is rife. So many people are scared, especially during dark times like recessions and, in more recent times, global pandemics, that there is not enough to go around.

Considering that I have become homeless during a recession and then made over six figures during a recession, I can safely say that how well you fare has nothing to do with the economic climate. It has everything to do with what you have in place from a business structure point of view and how much fear you allow in your heart and your head.

Success leaves clues and bees do this majestically. Of course, they do.

Here's how it goes down in Bee Town.

A little bee goes out foraging and looking for flowers, flowers that have enough pollen and nectar to make it worthwhile for other bees to come foraging and collecting from too.

Upon finding the good stuff, the bee goes back to the hive and, by the medium of dance, no less, tells the other bees where said good stuff is.

The little bee does not keep all the good stuff for itself. It finds where there is plenty for the rest of its pals and goes back and tells them.

Not only this, but bees also make sure that they do not entirely strip this area of all its pollen and nectar resources, so that stores can be replenished more quickly and that they may revisit again and again.

No scarcity here.

Here's the thing about success and abundance. Contrary to popular belief, there IS enough to go round if you allow yourself to believe and also if you box clever.

The media sells fear – the more salacious the better, especially around the economy. Stop tapping so much into that fear-driven mentality. Papers do not sell by telling you that everything is fine, and there are ways out of tricky situations. Instead, I implore you to be more bee and go seek the opportunities that are there.

Rest assured that you will know about the things you need to know when they come a-knocking. Get the eff off your backside and find the good stuff. When you do, you are most welcome to come over to The IATQB Hive and do a little happy dance!

Festooning

When I read about festooning in bees, I let out an excited squee. (Please tell me I'm not the only person in the world that does this.)

When bees are building something new in their hives, they link arms. They create lace-like frames to show the other bees that are busy building where to build to. WTF, right? I know.

Linking arms with people within our business communities is super powerful. We get to lift up one another and help show newer members where to build to and what is possible. Magic.

It was from this behaviour that I drew inspiration when I created my first significant charity endeavour to date, The Big Festoon. More on that later.

Positively Charged Goals.

Bees, when they are flying around, because of the way they flap their little bee wings, become positively charged. This happens because of how fast the bee bumps into charged particles, like dust, in the air.

On clear days, the petals on flowers are often negatively charged.

When the bee flies near the negatively charged flower, the two are attracted. Sparks don't fly, but pollen sometimes does, and the bee can tell that the flower is suitable for foraging from.

Once the bee has collected what it needs, the flower becomes neutrally charged and the other bees foraging in the area will sense this and avoid them, thus saving them time.

What a lush way of thinking about our own goals. When you set your goals with total clarity, it will feel like you and the goal are magnetised in much the same way.

I find the beauty in this behaviour glorious.

The more I learn about bees, the more I love them.

Being the Queen Bee is about leading a community. Audiences and clients love being a part of something, so I created The IATQB Hive, and the overall movement, as a safe space for people both new to business and those that have more time served to share their challenges and their successes. Success leaves clues, remember?

The IATQB Hive is a place where we waggle dance, festoon and swarm our way to success and I can't think of better role models than our stripy bumble-bummed pals.

BEING A CYCLE BREAKER

As an avid user of social media, particularly Facebook and Instagram, I come across inspirational quotes a lot.

I am guilty of screen-shotting my favourites and posting them on my timeline with a very self-important 'THIS.'

Behold, ye followers, this wisdom that is not mine that I am bestowing upon your feed! May your life be forever changed!

It rarely is. These memes are food for thought, at best; at worst, they are a cringe-fest. (If you haven't done this, by the way, and you are a millennial, I question your millennial status.)

This year though, I came across a quote that genuinely stopped me in my tracks.

This one floored me.

> **"Never underestimate a cycle breaker. Not only did they experience years of generational trauma, but they stood in the face of the trauma and fought to say, 'This ends with me.' This is brave. This is powerful. This comes at a significant cost. Never underestimate a cycle breaker."**
>
> **— NATE POSTLETHWAIT**

When I look back and really study the generations that came before me, poverty, domestic abuse, addiction and even obesity had been handed down to me, my sister and my cousins like a shitty gift that no one wants for Christmas.

My grandparents on my dad's side lived in the old mill terraces that were the former accommodation for local mill workers in Preston. They would shut my dad in the house when he was as young as three years old, for him to fend for himself while they went to the pub down the road to spend their benefit money.

Their arguments were explosive, and although a relatively slight man in stature, my grandad, Charles (known as

Chick), had a terrible temper in drink, as did my grandma, Rita, and between them, they were a perfect storm.

Drink featured heavily in the relationship and, of course, this informed a large part of my dad's own relationship with alcohol. Alcohol was an ever-present entity in Dad's world, so it is no surprise that it became a feature in his future relationships too.

I wish to be super clear, at this point, that I do not believe my grandparents nor my dad were terrible people. They didn't know any better, and so they didn't do any better. Times were very different back then, and families did not have the same language around mental health and coping mechanisms as we do now.

Where my grandparents were from, geographically, historically, societally and generationally, people did what they could to get by getting by, which often meant getting pissed.

Living from paycheck to paycheck and often living outside of their means by getting doorstep loans from high-interest community loan sharks and bar tabs meant that there was never any money in savings or even, sometimes, to put food on the table.

You can see why, when Dad got older, he struggled himself to make ends meet. He didn't have a clue what to do with money so he never really had any, or what he did make, he found hard to keep. His inherent generosity on the odd occasion when he *did* have money was a symptom of his unease with it.

My maternal grandparents were the same, but different.

My grandad, Eric, was a military man. My grandma, Irene (known as Rene), travelled with him from base to base while bringing up their five children, my mum being the final of these children – a happy accident that my grandma thought to be early onset menopause, in her late 30s.

They eventually settled in Preston in the mid-sixties. Accounts made by my mum and other family described my grandad, at the time, as brusque at best, grumpy and unloving at worst. He needed routine and order for him to be happy, and my mum found this incredibly restrictive as she was growing up.

Rene worked hard to make ends meet when Eric was away with work to provide for the children. Eric's only real concern was paying the household bills, so it was up to Rene to provide everything else.

Money was hard-won. It was hard to come by, and of course, drinking featured heavily.

The marriage came to an end when Eric had an affair. He would disappear like clockwork most evenings and weekends, and eventually, Rene caught wind of his infidelities, and they divorced.

Mum and Dad met and married young, both escaping their parents' messy lives but carrying, of course, their own respective wounds that they ultimately had no awareness of, language for, or capacity to heal from.

It is no surprise that, as the years wore on, the generational burden each of them carried around money, self-worth and drink became problematic.

The fights were as monumental as they were traumatic for my sister and me to witness.

They eventually divorced when I was sixteen. I was always confused as to why my mum stayed so long. She said she stayed because of my sister and me. Looking back, I find it beyond sad to think that she made decisions that held her back from happiness, while at the same time exposing us to the kind of toxicity that would go on to inform so many of my shitty choices later on in life.

It was a misplaced sacrifice.

When it got to my own relationships with money, men and career choices, it should have come as no surprise that I too made many poor decisions.

People like us didn't go on to make real money.

People like us weren't successful.

We didn't have big houses and epic, life-fulfilling jobs.

No wonder, when I started to make these things happen for myself, that the people around me got pretty uncomfortable. Not because they didn't love me, but because they couldn't keep me safe in this new space. It was so alien to them.

No wonder also that, when I first attempted to free myself and really go for the things I desired and the life that I truly wanted, that I sabotaged myself in many, many ways.

It was only when I realised that I was carrying the burden of generations of learned behaviour, that I was able to wake the fuck up and start to address what was actually happening.

It takes strength and power, and yes, sometimes comes at significant cost.

But I promise it is worth it.

The message here is that you are not your parents.

You are not your grandparents.

Or their parents.

You get to say, **'This ends with me.'**

And that is powerful as fuck.

If the only gift I can give my daughters, or indeed you, lovely reader, is this, I will consider my life a success.

In the following pages, I will share with you some of the things I did to help me begin to free myself of all that generational crappiness and how you can too.

SELF-SABOTAGE

I'M SAT HERE HAVING SO FAR written this book in sequence, and I have hit a wall. It has me frozen, hands poised above the keyboard, in a 'Where the hell do I begin?' spiral of anxiety.

The fear of sharing the things that I have done to cheat on my own success and happiness over the years has led me to all kinds of distractions to avoid writing this chapter.

Facebook, housework (which will be a ludicrous thought to those that know me) and phone calls checking in with my family have all featured in my avoidance.

It is a perfect example of the procrastination I have been plagued with for years. Self-sabotage and I have been uneasy bedfellows for as far back as I can remember.

The generations of conditioning around money, success, health and happiness or, more painfully, lack thereof, had left me yearning for them yet, in a surreal pantomime of events, saw me steal any chance I had of creating them from myself.

Our mind and our body's sole job is to keep us away from harm. To help us decide what risks to take in order to keep us alive. If the risk of something outweighs our potential to survive, it will often cause us to swerve the risk.

We experience this very viscerally in the form of our physical reaction to perceived threats – the fight-flight-freeze-fawn response.

When we understand this, we can start to dig a little deeper as to why we so very often get in our own way, especially when it comes to levelling up or attempting new things.

Let's look at the four responses and what happens when we experience them:-

Fight – Body perceives danger and tackles danger head-on, often with aggression.

Flight – Body perceives danger and flees the situation.

Freeze – Staying exactly where you are, moving as little as possible until the threat passes.

<u>Fawn</u> – This is often a trauma response and will manifest itself in the form of people-pleasing, being unable to say no and feeling unable to express our needs. It is one of the less talked about responses but one of the most significant ways we, particularly women, self-sabotage.

All of these responses are, almost always, acts of desperation. I mean, if you were chill about a situation, you would just calmly navigate your way through it, right?

I found myself in the throes of all of these stress responses in most areas of my life and often for extended amounts of time.

It was exhausting.

Fawning is what I did in the majority of my work and romantic relationships. Such was my desperate need to be seen, liked and loved, paired with an intense fear of conflict, that it saw me become the ultimate 'Yes Woman'.

Being the youngest sibling and coming from a veritable gaggle of cousins coming to stay with us growing up, each with their own intense struggles that my parents would try to help them with, I found myself craving attention.

I knew that making people feel good about themselves was a way of helping myself feel significant, even if it was to my detriment.

I didn't express my needs within relationships as I was just glad that someone gave enough of a shit about me to spend time with me. This led to several toxic friendships and work situations.

This took a dire turn for the worse when I found myself in the abusive romantic relationship I told you about earlier. I was transported back to being a child, and I would say and do anything to avoid arguments or continuously try to convince him to stay by over-giving.

If I could make him love me, he that finds me ultimately unlovable, surely that would make me worthy?

I would give him money. I bought him a car. I got into ridiculous debt. I even forgave his countless infidelities in the name of trying to be lovable.

This fawning came from a place of deep trauma from watching my parents, aunties, uncles and grandparents as a child, and consequently, this brought with it a pitiful lack of self-worth. I had no one to role model for me what a healthy relationship looked like.

I didn't stand a chance.

In staying, I was carrying on the generational cycle of abuse. Grotesquely, I stayed because it was all I truly knew how to deal with. You go to the man who is most like your father, right?

Eventually, with the help of a court order and my fantastic support network, we parted ways, and I found my way into the safe arms of my big, teddy bear of a husband today.

God love him, I was a bit of a state from a mental health perspective when we met, but he held space for me and loved me while I set about learning to love myself.

He saw the Queen in me long before I did.

The Flight in me manifested itself from a young age. I would be out of the house as much as I possibly could, hanging out with friends on the streets and parks and staying over at their houses on sleepovers as much as the other mums would let me.

As soon as I was able when I was sixteen, I left home. I moved in with a boyfriend, both of us too young to make the kind of commitment needed to co-habit in any practical way. The relationship quickly turned sour, and I moved back home for a short time.

Not long after this, I got on a plane to my first paid job outside the UK. It is only on reflection around this time that it is clear that I was running away as far as possible from life at home.

Although an enjoyable experience, this served to alienate me from those closest to me.

This Flight response became a way that I would self-sabotage to keep myself safe. (That's what these responses are designed for, right?)

To avoid conflict in my relationships, particularly with my husband, who is the safest and most lovely guy you could meet, I would run. I would go quiet, retreat and sometimes even go and stay in a hotel for a few days in an attempt to put distance between us instead of seeking solutions.

For me, conflict in a relationship meant violence, both physical and emotional and my mind and body would gear me up to avoid it at all costs. Removal of myself from stressful situations meant that I was clear of danger even when no real danger was on the cards.

This conditioned response almost cost me my marriage until I figured out what was happening, and now, we resolve our conflicts in a safe and more healthy manner.

The Freeze in me shows up as fatigue or procrastination. It rears its head every time I am heading for new levels of success.

I would set my sights on bigger and better things for myself and my family, and I set about trying to make them happen.

No sooner had I made the decision, something odd would occur. The housework suddenly looked fabulously appealing, or Facebook got super exciting, or I would get so damn tired and overwhelmed that I would promise myself that I would get started, I would... Right after this nap or after I google how tall Jesus was or something else equally as ludicrous.

Success was not something that I knew. It certainly wasn't something that my subconscious had any clue how to deal with. With this great unknown outcome in mind, success and all its trappings became a threat. A risk from which my mind and my body could not determine if they could keep me safe should I proceed.

Achieving success, health, wealth and happiness would require me to do things differently. It would require sacrifice. It would mean leaning into fear and yes, that made me very, very uncomfortable.

Freezing in this way had me doing the equivalent of what we discussed right at the beginning of the book in Chapter One. Things would look difficult or complicated, and I would take to my bed.

I would stand at the bottom of these proverbial mountains and think 'Fuck that!'

Of course, again, on waking up quite literally to the fact that I was sabotaging myself, I put on my big-girl pants and started to make some moves.

Knowledge and understanding of your self-sabotaging behaviours is the first step towards ownership and recovery of them.

The Fight in me shows itself in relentless workaholism.

Such was my fear of not having money, particularly after I became homeless, I would fill my diary with *any* work I could lay my hands on. Low value, high volume work exchanging time for money until there was no spare time to breathe and a total lack of self-worth around my value.

In my first few years of business, it was not unusual for me to take on up to eight gigs over a weekend (Thursday to Monday are typically a performer's workweek). These stints would chew me up and spit me out, leaving me barely able to function on my two 'days off'. I say 'days off' because there were no days off. The days not singing or driving to gigs were spent working on filling my diary with more and more work just to keep the proverbial wolf from the door.

I remember most weekends, falling through the door, often at three or four am, in tears because I was just so tired with little time to get my shit together before I had to be up with the kids.

The energy required to perform for extended periods is draining, to say the least, and this also took its toll.

I was heading straight for burnout, both physically and mentally. The price I was paying and the sabotage I was committing was to my health and my wellbeing.

It took me a while to recognise that I was in 'Fight' mode. In fact, it took me practically making myself ill to take stock and realise that in reality, I didn't need to fight so hard any more.

I am talented in my field, and as such I needed to at the very least charge my worth, so I didn't have to take on such low paying work.

Doing something so bold (in my mind, given my relationship with money) as putting my prices up, instantly allowed me the space to catch my breath and plan my next move which was to be the creator of IATQB.

Looking back, I want to take hold of Past Dani and give her a shake.

Of course, I can't, but I **can** love her, and I do, fiercely.

She grew strong. She became self-aware. She did the work, and she got us here.

What a fucking Queen.

I want to make her see how incredible she is: alas, unless I find a DeLorean and a wild-haired time-travelling scientist, that is not a possibility.

Knowing the things that I do now about Past Dani, however, and safe in the knowledge that Future Dani is gonna look back on Now Dani and love her just as much as Now Dani loves Past Dani, I finally feel the worthiness that I was seeking from outside of myself.

I now know that I can love Future Dani with all my heart. She has my back, and I am stronger and better equipped to navigate this road to success in a much less desperate and a much more love-filled way.

I want you to check in with your own fight-flight-freeze or fawn behaviours. Have they become ways to keep yourself 'too safe'?

Are you fighting where you don't need to?

Are you people-pleasing to avoid rocking the boat?

Are you running away from doing the things that make you happy if you only allow yourself to stand firm?

Are you standing still, waiting for the opportunities to land in your lap so that when they don't you can blame the lack of opportunities and not yourself?

It's time to call bullshit to that behaviour.

We carry around with us all this heavy stuff, right from our childhood. Our experiences, both good and bad, shape how we see the world, and it's not always helpful.

We forget that we CHOOSE to carry this burden.

Think about the past as a suitcase full of your previous experiences. It's like we all get given a suitcase and every bad thing that happens to us is a steaming pile of shit.

We instinctively, upon receiving this turd, pick it up and put it into our suitcase, and we carry it around with us.

Bad relationship? Into the turd case.

Put on weight or drank too much because you were self-soothing some trauma? Double turds for you, my friends.

Got sacked from a job...? Get a turd in that bag.

So, we're carrying around this shitcase, sorry, *suitcase* and it gets heavier and smellier the longer we hold on to it.

We can be guilty of putting this steaming suitcase at the feet of our newest relationships and ask the person we are now with why our case smells so damn terrible.

Often, in return, you get their case of crap and that can be equally smelly.

Worse, you can be jealous that they have somehow managed to get to this point with just a few rabbit poos and you find it unfair.

We end up tied up in a mess of blaming each other for our own shit!

We hold on to our shit.

We hold on to our trauma, be that clothes that don't fit any more, debt letters, cards from exes from happier times and so on.

For me, it was letters and court documents from when I lost my house and receipts from the wedding I had paid for that didn't go ahead. It was the non-molestation order issued against the man who had abused me.

It was the unsent letters I had written to my dad trying to make him see the pain he had caused.

If you are holding on to a big old bag of poo, you're carrying around some serious negative energy, and I shit you not (pardon the pun), that shit is affecting all your future outcomes.

We are in the business of success, and in order to #FlyAny-way, you have to be willing to let some shit go.

Here's how.

Thank that shit. Had it not been for it, all of it, you wouldn't be where you are now, and you are about to do some incredibly good shit from here on in. Be grateful for it.

Get rid of shit. If you have held on to physical stuff longer than you need, get a skip and throw that shit away. There are no pockets in shrouds, Darling; there is nothing that you can take with you, so it is important not to burden yourself with too much 'stuff'.

Decluttering is proven to free up emotional bandwidth, and it feels great afterwards. I promise.

It's like Senekot for the soul.

Release the shit. If you're able and it is safe to do so, have a burning ceremony, particularly for the stuff that has caused you real pain.

If you don't have any physical items, take some time and write down what happened and how it made you feel. Then get one of those cheapy wood burner things for the garden and burn the bugger. Have a dance around the fire as it burns and you release your shit to the heavens for added fun.

I want to see you hitting my socials with pics and vids of you dancing around wood burners, throwing stuff in skips, taking your crap to the tip and getting shot of your shit!

Make Future You proud because you paved the way for them.

They love you. Be flipping respectful, love them back and be more mindful of what you're doing to build the path to them.

DADDY ISSUES

A LESSON IN FORGIVENESS

IF SOMEONE HAD TOLD me years ago that forgiveness was the key to unlocking your ability to quit self-sabotage and to fly anyway, I would have explored this a long, long, looooong time ago.

> " **"Forgiveness is to set a prisoner free and to discover that the prisoner was you."**
>
> — **LEWIS B. SMEDES**

It was 8 am on the 10th of February 2016 when I got the call.

It was a call, I guess, I had been waiting on for some time.

'Your Dad's in hospital.'

Prior to this moment, I'd had little contact with my dad for about six years.

After he and Mum split, Dad went on to marry again: a lovely lady who remains a part of my family to this very day despite Dad's abhorrent behaviour that led to their, his second, divorce.

Following that, Dad left the area to pursue a life, I assume, away from the pain of his misfortunes and mistakes, of which there were many.

The difficulty with this was that his demons were never too far behind him and they showed themselves whenever he drank, which most of the time, was every day.

Once my sister and I began to have children of our own, we both decided that we couldn't subject them to Dad's erratic behaviour. He was like Jekyll and Hyde, and there was no way on this earth that we were going to have them confused by his duality.

Dad, by day, was a loving, kind, vivacious, master networker and much-loved member of the local community (frighteningly, in many ways, Dad and I are very similar). By night he was haunted by his inadequacies and feelings of worthlessness that he would project onto whoever was was closest to him at the time.

He languished in his victimhood whilst ploughing his way through tin after tin of strong lager and later, cheap cider. He would blame my mum, my sister and me, my grandma, my auntie and uncles and my cousins for all of his failings. His unhappiness was, of course, everyone else's fault except his own.

It wasn't always like this. When we were small, before the drink really took hold, I have a very different recollection of him.

Before the monster that my dad became, there was my Daddy.

He was the real deal, in my eyes. This was the man who would call me 'Princess' and 'Blossom' and blow-dried our hair on bath night. Instead of reading us bedtime stories, he would make up ridiculous tunes using the demo button on our little Yamaha keyboard.

I remember sitting on his knee and cuddling him whilst watching the TV late at night promising him that I would never be too grown up for snuggles. Back then, my Daddy was my safe person.

He was the slayer of the monsters under my bed and the spiders in the bathroom. He was the wiper of my tears when I was sad. He would wipe them from my face and put them in his pocket just in case he needed them later.

This version of my Dad was so excited by Christmas that he and Mum would make 'magic' happen for us that left Gemma and me squealing with delight.

One Christmas Eve, when Gem and I were fast asleep, he and Mum gently lifted us from our bed to theirs and decorated both of our bedrooms. We were placed back into our beds before we woke in the morning, both he and Mum feigning equal measure shock and surprise when we ran into them yelling, 'He's been! He's been!'

We must have been perhaps seven or eight years old when Gemma and I witnessed our first drink-fuelled family brawl that then shattered the Daddy illusion and initiated us into the complex world of coping with an alcoholic parent.

As we grew from children to teenagers, my sister and I became fed up with what was happening and would often defend Mum when Dad had too much to drink and began picking a fight.

Things were dark and stormy for this whole eight or nine year period, and I grew both angry and saddened by the person I found my Daddy to be.

When he eventually left and met his lovely second wife, his behaviour remained. He was far too lost in his demons to admit that there was a problem, and this relationship ended a few years later.

It was then that I decided that it was best for all involved that we have no further contact.

I was heartbroken by the fact this guy just didn't bother to show up for himself or for his kids. This supposed 'pillar of the community' found it impossible to do the right thing and fight for his children and grandchildren.

I was jealous of the people that had lovely dads. I felt robbed.

In my late teens, I realised that the apology that I was owed was never going to come and that knowledge sat inside my chest and burned.

The feeling of unworthiness that his parents had given him, he had now passed down to me, and this showed up, as we have talked about at length, in so many of the shitty parts of my life.

Dad had been involved in an accident. He had slipped on a broken step at the holiday site that he was managing at the time, and he had suffered a catastrophic brain injury.

As I sat in the car on the way to the hospital, I recounted the six peaceful years that had just passed and was furious with my dad that the only time I heard about him was when he was bringing more turmoil to my life.

I waited outside the doors to ICU at Royal Preston Hospital for the surgeon to come and speak with me.

My sister had decided that she wasn't going to attend. She had dealt with Dad by forgetting he even existed, and by coming to the hospital, she would have had to uncover wounds that had long since been buried.

The surgeon explained that I might not recognise my dad due to the amount of swelling he had all over his body and the bruising to his face from both the fall and the surgery to remove the shattered front part of his skull.

He also explained that, due to the nature of the injury, if he were to survive at all, he would most likely be left in a vegetative state.

I called Gems to update her, and she asked what I thought she should do. I told her, based on what the medical team were telling me, this was probably the last time she would have the chance to see him, and she would regret it if she didn't come.

As we were at his bedside, Dad, swollen, bruised beyond recognition, ventilated and covered in tubes and us, wild-eyed and afraid of what was to come, we were presented with a choice.

Walk away and allow whatever was about to unfold to do so with no further involvement from us. After all, we owed this man nothing.

Or stay.

Stay and do what was needed of us as his daughters and see to it that this person who we did not really know any more was cared for regardless of the outcome.

In making this decision to stay, we were both all in.

We hauled shifts at the hospital, making sure one of us was always at his side keeping a vigil by his bed just in case he came out of his coma, which, as the days passed, became more and more unlikely.

Ivy was just a baby at the time, and I was still breastfeeding. I remember the eerie stillness of the ward whilst I fed her. The whole room was stuck in the purgatory of gravely ill and injured people not knowing who was going to live or die around us.

After two weeks of this, the doctors quietly and gently told us that there was little more they could do for Dad and as such, the following day, they were going to begin the end of life pathway and that we should contact anyone who may wish to say goodbye.

We duly did as we were told and it was scheduled that at around 7 pm the following evening, the tubes and machines keeping Dad alive would be removed and he would pass away.

My sister and I arrived at the hospital at around 11 am the next morning, clinging to the hope that maybe a miracle would happen. I sat at the end of his bed and rubbed his feet as I had for the past couple of weeks whilst we both talked to him.

A nurse came over to speak with us about what was going to happen over the course of the evening, what to expect etc. and she touched his shoulder telling us that she was really sorry that they couldn't do any more when I saw, for the first time, Dad tried to open his eyes!

She initially dismissed it as an involuntary nervous reaction, but we were having none of it. We asked for the doctor, and Dad clumsily opened one eye again.

The miracle we were holding out for, it seemed, had indeed occurred.

Dad very slowly awoke from his coma and thus began the long and arduous process of rebuilding him.

The next eighteen months were spent at his bedside trying to help him come to terms with life with such a severe brain injury.

It was like he'd had a devastating stroke. He was right-side dominant, and the left side of his brain that controlled it was mush. He was now the child, and we were now the parents.

Four years on, Dad now resides in a care home near to us, and we visit regularly.

Aside from his physical disabilities (he is unable to walk and his right side has seized almost entirely), Dad struggles with his communication and capacity to make decisions to keep himself safe.

That said, he knows what he wants to say even if he struggles to find the words. Just like having a baby, Gemma and I became well versed in 'Dad', and as he made more progress, albeit slow, his speech came back to a level where he could make himself understood.

He would ask us to go through old photos of the family, so Mum, who supported all of our decisions regarding Dad, dug out old photographs and tapes for us to show him.

One such tape was a VHS of a shaky camcorder recording of our street's celebration of Preston Guild in 1992. The video charted the inhabitants of the cul-de-sac where we grew up getting ready for the street party that my mum and dad had helped to organise.

Both Gemma and I and all of the children from the street were there in fancy dress, including my cousins who lived with us at the time. Friends and family from a time when my dad was my Daddy all came onto the screen, fading in and out like ghosts.

And there was my Dad.

It was a long-standing joke at the time that he looked like Super Mario and he had dressed accordingly for his fancy dress. It was both strange and heart-breaking to see him clowning around for the camera. I began to cry.

I cried for everything we could have had as father and daughter and everything we would never have now, even though we were together most days.

Dad and I sat side by side, him in his wheelchair and me on my plastic, hospital issue chair, and he held my hand while my face leaked big, fat, ploppy tears.

He looked at me and wiped them away as he once did when I was small.

He asked me what was wrong and I told him that was probably the last memory I had of us all being happy.

He held my hand again and quietly looked back to the TV, the screen showing my mum dressed as a teapot, playing jump rope with some of the kids.

'I know,' he said quietly. 'I am sorry.'

Having come back from rock bottom myself and having done much of the subsequent inner work as part of my own personal development journey, I knew that my dad did what he could at the time with the only tools he knew. In his case, the tool was drinking to mask a childhood of rejection and a lifetime of feeling unworthy.

This knowledge couldn't stop the little girl in me from being robbed of her Daddy, but it did allow me to truly forgive him long before I received the apology.

It was in a similar awakening that I was able to forgive my older children's biological fathers. They were carrying their own pain, and it was not my responsibility to absolve them of any wrongdoing.

It was my job to free *myself* from the pain of carrying around the injustice that I had experienced.

I also had to forgive myself. I had made all the decisions at each stage of my life with the knowledge and the tools I had at the time.

In a similar way to my father, albeit with different ways of coping, I had worn my victimhood like a badge of honour, and I was sick of it holding me back. It was a heavy and unnecessary burden.

So now, as I know better, I do better.

Forgiveness is not something that you do for other people to exonerate them of their misdemeanours, it is something you do for *yourself* to stop you drinking the bitter poison of hate and expecting it to harm the other person.

Why am I telling you all this, my lovely reader?

I want you to take a second to consider your own situations.

Are you burdened by the weight of shit you can't change or control?

Are you carrying around anger at yourself or someone else and it is no longer serving you?

You can CHOOSE to release yourself from it.

When you do, you create bandwidth in your life to grow more abundantly. It's like getting rid of the thorny ugly brambles out of a garden to make way for beautiful flowers.

I did tell you some of this stuff wouldn't be easy, but it is so worth it.

I started moving towards the incredible stuff I do now when I stopped trying to navigate my way forward by looking in the rear-view mirror.

Forgiving yourself is one of the hardest things to do. I remember beating myself up for all manner of things like:

Why did I stay in such toxic relationships for so long?

Why could I never seem to keep hold of money when I had it?

How could someone as intelligent and self-aware as me get into such shitty situations?

I was the common denominator in all of my failings, and it was tough giving myself a break.

Here's how I got to grips with it:

There is a beautiful Hawaiian practice of reconciliation and forgiveness called Ho'oponopono. It is a method that can be practised in many ways and in many relationship variants, including the relationship with oneself.

It truly allowed me to take back control and relinquish any shame or guilt I felt.

The practice is split into four stages.

1 - Repentance/Saying I'm Sorry – Now then, this is not me all of a sudden getting all religious on you. Whether religion is your bag or not, saying you're sorry, even to yourself, is crucial.

I was so sorry that I had deprived myself of happiness. I was sorry that I wasn't, in many ways, showing up as well as I could for my family. There were many reasons I felt sorry, and this practice allowed me to accept this. The intention is not, however, to unpack and dwell here.

Once you have identified the things that you are sorry for, you can move to the next stage.

2 – Forgiveness – Asking for forgiveness, especially from yourself, gives you the power to let go of the pain you have been inflicting upon yourself. When you offer yourself forgiveness, you are permitting yourself to release all the crap you have been carrying around. Ask yourself 'Please forgive me' and, more importantly, allow yourself to answer 'Yes.'

3 – Gratitude – Expressing gratitude or saying 'Thank you' honours the release that you have just granted. Fear, anger, remorse and pain cannot exist in the same space as gratitude. I am grateful to myself and everything that has happened to me every day. All paths have led me here. All roads have brought me to you, Dear Reader. What's not to be grateful for?

4 – Love – Of course. To truly love ourselves again is beyond powerful and an incredible platform from which to spring forward.

Give it a go.

When we know better, we do better.

Sending you a big squishy hug, that was some heavy shit.

～

I want to take a second to shout out to all the dads out there who show up. You fabulous humans are what we need more of in the world. There are good men in existence, and I am a fan.

WEEDS AND WISHES

SINCE EMBARKING on my IATQB quest, my youngest daughter, Ivy, has been a regular feature on my live streams. She often pops up on my morning Facebook show, all sleepy-eyed and bed-headed, to say good morning to our guest and viewers.

She has become quite the little star.

At the time of writing this, Ivy is four years old and full of four-year-old insights that sometimes are so profound/funny/wise that I cannot help but share.

Some of the things she does, like singing the wrong words to songs (her renditions of 'We're All Going On An Alcoholiday' and 'Blah, Blah, Black Sheep' are my particular favourites), dressing up as a pirate to get her pre-school vaccinations because pirates say 'Arrrr' and not 'Ow', or the time she had a sore throat and a 'beaver' has us unable to maintain a straight face when she is being deadly serious.

More recently, Ivy has taken to using the word 'Poo' as a term of endearment for us.

Not in an affected way. It sounds dead natural and throw-away.

'Morning, Poo!'

'See you later, Poo!'

'Love you, Poo!'

I said to her, 'Ives, why are you calling everyone Poo?'

She said (without missing a beat), 'Because they are, so it seems appropriate.'

It is not the kind of logic that I can argue with.

She calls business cards my 'Busyness Cards' because when I give them out, I get busy.

I mean, this kid KNOWS the score.

Four-year-olds see things in the most innocent and fabulous ways. Their imagination knows no bounds and the whole world is a playground.

Walking to the shop with her, however, takes bloody ages.

She wants to feel EVERY surface on the way, or talk to the cats and dogs we see to ask where its mummy is or smell every single flower we come across, just in case one daffodil smells different to the next, and she wouldn't want to miss out.

Being one of life's 'busy' people, it's hard not to get frustrated. I'm trying to get shit done. I'm moving at a million miles an hour, and sometimes it's hard to remember that it is important to pause.

Ivy really does make me pause. She is an incredible reminder that there is joy to be found on the journey, not just at the destination.

One of the most profound lessons that Ivy taught me was on a sunny Tuesday last year as we were leaving the house for the school run.

The morning, so far, had been spent refereeing Poppy and Daisy because they are at the age in siblinghood where it is a crime for one of them to do so much as dare even breathe the same air as the other.

Poppy had had a full-on, pre-teen meltdown over the atrocity of there being no appropriate cereal in the house (there were three boxes of varying types). Daisy had been in tears because there was some art project that I should have helped her with weeks ago due in that morning of which I had no knowledge as she hadn't told me.

To top off the carnage, the dogs saw fit to, both of them, find their way upstairs and take two of the most ungodly shits in the kids' bedroom.

I was stressed, to say the least.

I finally, with minutes to spare before I became THAT mum at school that is shamed by the receptionist for daring to bring my offspring to *their* entrance as the class doors were now closed, got the two older girls out of the front door.

I exited the house and was affronted by the vision that was before me.

The house where we currently live was the house that we moved into after we became homeless. Our very kind land-lords allowed us to move in with little notice and the house at the time was a roof over our heads, which was exactly what we needed.

The area that the house is in, however, is not the most desir-able. We have been plagued through the years with various groups of ASBO type, idiot teenagers harassing us. From throwing eggs and rotten fruit at the house to putting the windscreens through on our cars and slashing our tyres.

One time, they even graffitied large, rudimentary penises on all of our fence panels (I both laughed and cried at this).

The reason that I was affronted was not because of any of this, but because it was the end of dandelion season.

Because we were not particularly enamoured with where we were living, looking after the garden had not been high on the priority list. As such, the front lawn was not only overgrown but literally hundreds of white-headed dandelions had sprouted, seemingly overnight.

I was fuming. A whole blanket of weeds lay before me. I looked in dismay at the hundreds of tiny dandelion bombs ready to go off and infect the whole damn street with more weeds. These were obviously sent by the God of Crappy Gardens specifically to torment me and remind me of my inadequacies with regards to keeping a house.

I called Ivy out to come and get in the car. The older two were cross-armed, taut-lipped and looking out of their respective windows because God forbid one should look out of the other's window.

Ivy came outside as I locked the front door, internally seething at my husband for putting off mowing the damn lawn.

She gasped.

Her eyes widened, and she jumped up and down in excitement. She was made up. So joyful was she that she could barely get her words out for a second.

'Mummy!' she cried, 'Mummy LOOK! Look at all these wishes in the garden. I'm so happy! I get alllll these wishes!!! Aren't we lucky?!'

And that's it, isn't it?

We, all too often, go through life thinking about all the adulting that we need to do. We get lost in the seriousness of it all.

We forget to play.

We forget to see the wishes in the weeds.

We learn most through play, and it is so much more fun than just allowing your lessons to come from your adversities, damn it.

We could all do to be a bit more Ivy.

So, what'll it be, my lovely friends?

When the drudgery of life is hanging heavy, are you going to look for weeds or wishes?

There is so much joy to see if only we allow ourselves.

I know which I prefer.

SHIT SHOES

FROM HERE ON IN, I'm going to share with you some of the stories, insights and learnings that I have gathered after that fateful night back in 2011 when I decided I was going stop being a victim and start happening to life instead of the other way round.

But before I do, I have a confession.

There is nothing particularly new or ground-breaking in these pages.

I am not special, no matter how much my mum tells me.

I have no magic formula for you to suddenly start farting glitter and making your millions.

I'm sorry to disappoint, but there is no new news.

A good friend of mine, mindset coach, Croz Crossley says –
'You can't skip the steps.' This applies wherever it is that
you are heading.

I am not going to share with you any shortcuts to your
health, wealth and happiness so if that is what you were
hoping for then you are probably better off finding a
certainty-selling type, regurgitating super-systems that will
have you pulling in seven figures quicker than you can say
'Shiesty'.

The concepts that I will share with you are taught and
shared in lots of different ways by lots of different people. I
will reference and signpost you to these glorious thought
leaders and change-makers as we go. I will most certainly
not take any credit for the teaching.

What I will do is share with you how I implemented these
concepts, and then I will hold space for you to give this
some thought too.

Holding space is an idea that I only really got to grips with
a couple of years ago.

I began reading personal development books when I was at
my lowest ebb. I was desperately seeking knowledge from
these guru-type humans who left the breadcrumb trail of
hope leading the way to ultimate success, happiness and all
the other good shit in the sure and certain hope that I could
achieve the same.

I would ask advice from all kinds of people, and my mind buzzed with various, and sometimes conflicting, information.

At this point, I was in no way in a position whereby I trusted myself yet. I was still a little raw from the roller coaster of the previous few years, and so I sought out my very first coach.

This coach came to me in the guise of my very dear friend, Heidi Mavir – The Unstoppable Woman. I had seen her via her live streams on social media and found the way she spoke compelling. I had never had a coach before, and I wasn't too sure what to expect.

During my time in the corporate world, I was fortunate to have been through lots of formal training around leadership skills and coaching, so the notion of coaching as a method was not new to me. In fact, I was a dab hand at it.

I had been known in both the training room and the board room to be able to get the most lost of causes back on track.

Taking the very advice and help I was giving and applying the same strategies that I would readily provide someone else with to my own life, however, was a tall order.

This was a case of the Cobbler's Shoes.

The story goes like this:

There was once a cobbler from a small village. He had built himself quite a reputation for being the best cobbler in the land.

Rich people and dignitaries from all over would come to the cobbler and have him make their shoes.

One day, when getting himself ready for another day keeping the hoi polloi well shod, the cobbler paused and realised that his own shoes were full of holes and in a pretty shitty state.

The cobbler, in looking after everyone else, had neglected his own needs.

I'm sure that those of you reading this will not find this analogy lost on you.

It was much the same for me: I had all this knowledge but none of the self-discipline, trust in my abilities or space to apply any of it.

I drove to Wakefield and sat down in Heidi's front room. She made me a coffee, and we began the process.

I was seeking answers and advice, remember? So you can imagine my discomfort when Heidi began asking me questions around what MY thoughts were on what the direction that my life should take.

What would **I** have to do and change in order to achieve that?

Who would **I** have to be?

Who would **I** have to surround myself with?

Who would **I** have to *stop* surrounding myself with?

What was my relationship with money like?

What did my self-care look like?

Suddenly, I was being asked to seek my own answers instead of seeking them from outside of myself. Heidi was teaching me to trust myself again by reminding me that I had the answers all along.

It was a lot, but it was necessary.

By leading me back to myself and allowing me the space to externalise and organise my thoughts where there was no judgement, only loving acceptance, Heidi unlocked the bit of me that I had forgotten.

That I was enough and that my intuition was a valid and intelligent force within me.

So, when I say there is no new news, there really isn't. You just need to hold enough space for yourself to remember who you the fuck you are.

The journey to becoming a Queen Bee was not about learning fancy systems, new ways to make money or build a business. That all came later when I had learned how to listen to myself and take myself seriously again.

It starts with YOU.

Because, my darlings, you simply cannot have shit shoes.

SHOW UP, WISE UP, RISE UP

To HELP us get into a position where we can move forward, to march onward into the reclamation of our birthrights of success and abundance, I thought it might be helpful if I shared with you what I do on a daily basis to make sure my life compass is calibrated and I'm on the right track.

In the corporate world, there are lots of snappy acronyms and diagrams to help get you working more effectively.

There is no end of talk of S.M.A.R.T. targets and WIIFM and F.A.B.... all manner of wanky jargon.

All these things are cool, I mean, I love a SMART Goal, but seeing as though I wanted to create a movement whereby I help people from all kinds of backgrounds Fly Anyway, I needed something more approachable and less... well, wanky. Something easy to remember and, most importantly, something that would apply to any area of life, not just business.

Business and life go hand in hand. If your life is a shambles, business will be hard work. Similarly, if your business is taking a nosedive, chances are, other areas of your life will be affected too.

Using the age-old concept of action, assessment and adjustment (I told you there's no new news here) paired with my knowledge of the things you need to lead a happy and abundant life, I created the... WAIT FOR IT...

THE IATQB SUPER-AWESOME 3 STAGE SUCCESS CYCLE!

Snappy, huh?

ANYONE can use this tool, no matter their start point, whether you are seasoned seven-figure earner or you are just beginning your foray into self-development.

Here's the tea.

First of all, I want you to think of the areas of your life that you want to work on. Here's a list of examples to get you started:

- Health
- Finances
- Relationships

- Family
- Network
- Giving Back
- Time
- Travel
- Business
- Purpose

This is just a starter for ten; you go ahead and pick which works for you.

Once you have your list, give each area a mark out of ten, ten being super awesome and zero being needs an intervention.

You also need to establish which of these things are important to you: it will be a waste of your time if you choose a category that you aren't arsed about improving.

Now for the snazzy diagram:

As you can see, there are three sections to the Super Awesome Success Cycle.

SHOW UP – WISE UP – RISE UP

Here I will break down what each section means and what to do for each.

SHOWING UP

To carve the path to where you want to be, you need to get real in terms of where you are right now.

For years I felt the sting of resentment that I wasn't taken seriously both in work and amongst my peers, or at least I didn't perceive myself to be.

SHOW UP, WISE UP, RISE UP

I would get angry when people didn't respect my boundaries or when people expected me to help them when they wouldn't offer me the same kindness.

When I finally got the sack from my corporate job, it had nothing to do with my abilities.

These things happened largely, if not entirely, because of how I was showing up.

I would be so over-giving of my time and energy to people who didn't matter to the point that they would take advantage. The thing is, I wasn't respectful of these things for myself, so why should they be?

When I was in more formal employment, I would do the absolute bare minimum of what was expected of me. I would submit what I had to and then mindlessly scroll the internet until my workday was done.

I hid from my team because they didn't respect me (I mean, why would they?). I would call in sick out of anxiety because I disliked the people that I worked with so much. It was no wonder that I found myself in disciplinaries for making the most stupid of mistakes. I would sabotage myself because I had no destination and also no desire to be there. It was making me desperately unhappy, and it showed.

When considering where you want to be, you have to look at how you need to show up in order to be there.

Does the person with a good and loving relationship with their kids negate spending time with them? Do they put pressure on them to behave a certain way or conform to unrealistic ideals?

Are these children given no boundaries or discipline for the sake of an easy life?

No! To have a positive relationship with your kids, you have to **Show Up** for them and hold the space for them that they need so that they can grow. You need to actively parent them, not just be their friend, or worse, have them believe that they are a burden.

Have a look at the areas of your life that you wish to work on and consider how you are showing up right now in that area.

Are you being who you need to be?

Are you being seen in the necessary places?

How are you presenting yourself to the world?

Are you doing what it takes in that area of your life to Rise Up?

What is your mindset really doing in this area?

This is the section of the cycle where you have to get real AF with yourself. If your goals are a destination in a sat nav, you need a start point as much as you need an end point.

WISING UP

If there is an area of your life where you have a goal that you have not yet attained, chances are you most likely are missing some information about it.

If you knew *everything* there was to know about your goal, it's most likely that you would have achieved it or be pretty close.

This includes the knowledge of oneself—more on that in a sec.

Having a goal is all well and good, but not doing the learning or taking the action necessary will mean that it will remain just that. A goal. A dream. Some fanciful situation where there are rainbows, butterflies, unicorns... and a distinct lack of you.

There will be a number of things that you may need to learn or Wise Up about to attain your goal and therefore Rise Up.

It could be as simple as creating a strategy – a set of actions that you need to complete to get you your destination.

It could be process related. As it stands, maybe you lack the systems that you need to do the work you need to do, and this may be stopping you from scaling, for example.

This was definitely the case in my business when I first started out in the online space.

My goal, amongst other things, was to turn over more profit.

First thing I had to Wise Up to was my money mindset. I had to unlearn the generations of lack and scarcity mentality. I set about healing my relationship with money, using a variety of different healing techniques. (A great book to read on this is Jen Sincero's You Are A Bad Ass At Making Money)

I had to learn to love money instead of being afraid of it.

Also, being somewhat of a technophobe meant that I was creating work for myself in the beginning. Not having the correct software in place meant that the time it was taking to reach my sales goals was much longer and much more difficult because I had no automation.

As such, I couldn't reach as many people and so didn't turn over as much profit.

By learning about the automation software that I required in order to scale, I was able to implement processes and systems to do that very thing.

In my first months of self-employment, I went to seek advice from my fantastic DJ friend and collaborator, Des Grant. I was worried that I had everything that I needed to create my singing business but the whole issue of paying my own tax and such scared me: after all, I had always been in 'safe' employment.

Des, in his infinite patience and wisdom, smiled and simply said, 'Dani, G.S.I.'

'I beg your pardon?' I asked, having no clue what he was suggesting.

'G.S.I.' he repeated. 'Get Someone In! If there is something you cannot do, them get someone in to help. Their expertise will save you both time and money. G.S.I.'

I hadn't even thought about it like that.

Investing in something, actually speculating to accumulate wasn't something I was used to, but is it a revelation when you do!

Wising Up may mean that you come to the awareness of your strengths but also your weaknesses. In doing this, you can identify if it is actually something that outsourcing will help with. I promise, it is worth it.

When identifying the areas in which you need to Wise Up, consider the mentors you may need, the friends you surround yourself with as well as the nuts and bolts stuff.

The people that you surround yourself with will have a direct impact on how quickly you progress towards any goal.

Wising Up helps you create the road map needed so that you can Rise Up.

Which brings us nicely to:

RISING UP

This is the really tasty bit of the whole thing.

This is the dream section.

You have established where you are right now, and now you are ready to consider a destination.

In the UK, there is a department store called Argos. For the past fifty years, Argos would publish a catalogue[1] containing every single thing that the store stocked. From watches and jewellery to garden furniture and everything in between.

Instead of going around a store with a trolley, you would flick through the catalogue and find the reference number of the item that you wanted. You then wrote the reference number on a little ticket using a red pencil (or a tiny blue pen in the posh stores) and took the ticket to the cashier.

Upon paying the cashier for your goods, you would be ushered to a waiting area to wait for your items to come from the warehouse.

The Argos catalogue was nicknamed 'The Book of Dreams'. Many a Christmas, my sister and I would get hold of Mum's copy of this veritable encyclopedia of stuff and circle what we wanted Father Christmas to bring us.

Suffice to say, our parents could not afford the invariably mile-long list of Kitty Kitty Kittens, Nintendos and Teddy Ruxpins that we suddenly *needed* upon seeing the pictures of happy kids playing with said delights in the catalogue. It did give us something to do in the excitement leading up to Santa coming and also gave Mum and Dad at least an idea of what they could get us.

I would love you to treat this section much like you would an Argos catalogue.

Imagine all of the things that you would like to achieve for the areas that you are working on to be a ten.

You may wish to obtain a pay rise in your job.

You might want to work on your marriage.

Your network may be sorely lacking, and as such you're playing small because you are surrounded by others who are playing small.

Take some time here to paint the picture: the clearer you are, the better here.

What does it REALLY mean to you to Rise Up in these areas?

Will you travel more? Will you have a bigger house? Will you have more time with your loved ones?

Then ask yourself, based on the last two sections:

How do you need to Show Up to achieve these things?

Where do you need to be seen?

Who do you need to Show Up for?

What EXACTLY do you need to do to Wise Up in these areas so that you can chart your course?

You will find that by putting all these things in place, you will get where you are going so much quicker than sitting on your arse hoping your dreams will just land in your lap by the power of thought alone.

As we discussed at the beginning of the chapter, you can apply this cycle to any area of your life at any time.

It is worth remembering that success, however you measure it, is not really a destination; it is an ongoing process.

Nobody ever stays at the top of Mount Everest, right?

When you have reached your goal, use the cycle to analyse where you landed, and then plot the next point in your journey.

And so on, and so on.

Join us in the IATQB Hive on Facebook and get accountable in there with us, if you need. I would love to know what your goals are and what you are learning along the way to smash them!

---

1. At the time of this book going to print, Argos have sadly announced that they are no longer printing the 'Book of Dreams'. Gemma and I both raised a glass to its departure and wondered how the heck we are going to let our Mum know what we want for Christmas this year. Sad times indeed.

CRABS

BEING a speaker who loves to entertain and educate at the same time, imagine my utter delight when I stumbled across of way of asking my audiences if they have crabs to raise a laugh whilst leading into a serious teach about who they surround themselves with.

When I do this in a talk, I finish a section (often, at this point, on imposter syndrome or similar) and then click my slide deck to a bold yellow slide with the words:–

'DO YOU HAVE CRABS?'

emblazoned across the screen.

It is worth the cackles from the naughty ones in my audiences every single time.

This doesn't work quite so well when I'm writing a book so you will just have to imagine my taking a cheeky pause waiting for everyone to catch up, giggle and settle again so we can learn some more cool stuff.

Crab Mentality or Crab Theory has, you will be pleased to know, nothing to do with sexually transmitted diseases and more to do with human behaviour.

When we went on our caravan holidays as kids, we would go crabbing. We would take our buckets, string and bits of bacon to the water's edge and see how many we could catch before setting them free again when we were done.

It is a notable phenomenon that when a crab is in such a container, if on its own, it will claw its way up and out of said container.

However, should you put more than one crab into a container and one attempts to escape, the other crabs in the bucket pull it back down.

The reason that crabs do this is often argued. On the one hand, it could be seen as hindering the absconding crab's escape; on the other, it may be that the other crabs can now see a means to get out themselves.

In an attempt to use the leverage that the escaping crab has, the other crabs hold onto it to attain some traction of their own, but the sides of such containers are often slippery and consequently, our little escaping crabby slips back down to the bottom and no one gets out.

This is a wonderful analogy for those of us who try to expand past their current situations and find the people around them struggle with the thought of it.

I've seen this behaviour, this 'Crab Mentality' in many different guises, both in my corporate career and also when I have tried to do things differently in life and business.

When I originally wanted to go into entertainment, particularly when I was exploring working outside of the UK, the people closest were very concerned.

Where would I live?

Would I have enough money to survive?

And so on, and so on.

When I was out there, after a while, this became:

'When would I be coming home?'

'You need to put down some roots.'

'Where is all this heading? Perhaps it's time for a proper job.'

It wears thin after a while and took lots of resolve to persevere.

Here's the thing: my friends and family didn't want me not to do well, it was just that my path was so very different from theirs that it felt to them that what I was doing was unsafe.

When I had truly begun my healing journey and started to make the necessary sacrifices with my time and energy so that I could create the life I truly wanted for my girls and me, old friends began to fall away because they couldn't understand the new, unbroken me.

They didn't know what to do with this ambitious, strong, dynamic woman on a mission or where she had come from.

I stopped being safe for them.

They were trying to pull me back to the safety of what they considered normal.

The problem was, I had become a different kind of crabby.

Chances are, if you are reading this, you're a different kind of crabby too.

I had a horrid experience in my entrepreneurial life where I confided in someone I thought was a friend in the online space. I told her of the plans I had and the strategy I intended on using.

Lo and behold, this friend became quiet and started to 'ghost' me.

A few short weeks later, this 'friend' had launched my whole concept.

This crab was trying to climb over me to catch their own break.

There are lots of ways that you may find this will show up for you as you begin to grow and change.

You may have set yourself a health goal, and now everyone around you is suddenly trying to convince you that you're perfect as you are and you really shouldn't be letting your health be your sole focus... there are more important things in life... like cake, right? (I mean, cake IS pretty important.)

You may have been working reeeeeaaalllly hard on your business to level up and all of a sudden, you're 'doing too much'.

You may have just bagged a dream job, but the crabbies in the office are mad because, of course, you didn't get that promotion fairly, your face just fit. (Assholes – Office Crabs are the WORST kind of crabs.)

You may have just made the leap from 'gainful employment' to full-time entrepreneurship and the nay-sayers are naying.

When you experience this, you are going to need to focus.

Get your eyes firmly on the prize and strengthen your resolve.

Just because something is not for the people around you does NOT mean that it is not for you.

If choosing better for yourself means making people around you uncomfortable, that's on them, NOT on you.

The best way to help yourself in this situation is to start getting really fucking picky about with whom you decide to spend your time.

A famous quote from American entrepreneur Jim Rohn goes –

> **"You become like the five people you spend the most time with. Choose carefully."**
>
> **— JIM ROHN**

If you are surrounding yourself with positive people who are all striving for better, it goes without saying that you will find it infinitely easier to do the same.

Go out there and curate your circle.

Surround yourself with the people you aspire to be like.

Find the other, different kind of crabbies who have already escaped the container; often, they will reach back to offer you a helping hand.

You can do this both on and offline. I'm a huge advocate of networking in both spaces and, after the more recent lockdowns and pandemic issues, it's not a bad idea to make sure that you have a presence in both spaces, especially if you are running a business.

Go seek out the groups that have leaders and communities that have similar values to you. People from which you can learn and also where you can bring your own value and experiences to the table too.

Your network is your net worth. Be sure to surround yourself with gold fucking bullion and not those smelly, awful crabs.

MENTORS

WISDOM COMES IN TWO FORMS – mistakes or mentors, and it is here that things get exciting.

We have spoken at length about how I had royally fucked things up for myself in the past. I want to share with you how I unfucked things up.

Fucking up is a reversible process, especially with the right guidance.

This guidance can, of course, come in the form of listening to your intuition, but sometimes, as in my case, you may not be ready to trust this just yet.

On the subject of who to surround yourself with whilst on your journey to success, the people who have climbed out of the bucket long before you – reaching back to give you a lift – are imperative to the speed and trajectory at which you will progress.

This is to say that, regardless of how driven we are, seeking the support of those who have overcome similar adversities to us and who are doing the thing we wish to do is guaranteed to assist your progress at a rate that far exceeds what it would be without doing so.

Success leaves clues, and many successful people have mentorship practices either within their business model or as a means of giving back.

By August 2018, I had created a successful (successful, at the time, meant our bills were paid and we weren't homeless any more) singing business. I was travelling up and down the country, performing in every kind of event you can imagine, from huge mayoral gala balls to social clubs.

Even though the work was plentiful, it was hard. I know that hard work is subjective and I do not wish to, in any way, downplay roles such as those within our NHS etc., but it was fucking tough.

A performer working on the circuit is a driver as their primary vocation, heavy goods lifter and sound engineer in the second instance and only then does performing play a role. Even then, the audiences are not the adoring fans I would dream of as a child.

It is not a glamorous life.

Possibly the least glamorous aspect of life on the road was the changing facilities in the venues, or more often than not, lack thereof.

From men's bathrooms to freezing cold beer cellars, getting ready for a gig can happen in the strangest of places.

After a couple of years of playing 'Changing Room Roulette', I decided that I would just get ready in my car. It was quiet, I would be undisturbed, and I could have the heating on if it got chilly (which in the north of the UK is a given most of the time).

As a means to keep myself entertained while I put my stage makeup on, I would live stream to Facebook and chat to whoever popped up. I would muse on what was happening in the news, what I had learned that week or what was happening in my world at the time.

There is something strange about people putting makeup on via live streaming; it can be quite compelling viewing, so it seems, and I would have people tuning in to my 'Get Ready With Me' lives regularly.

This was where IATQB began to form.

I knew that I was on to something. I knew that I was helping people by sharing these musings/teachings etc. online but I had no direction for it, and I was that burdened by the volume of performance work I was doing, that I couldn't see how to make more of it.

So, for years, I just carried on, building my audience via live stream with no clear direction but I loved on them so much, and they were great company for me whilst I was on the road, that I knew there was more for us as a collective.

It was around the summer of 2018 that I realised that I categorically did not want to be working in this relentless way any longer.

I hadn't had Bank Holidays or Christmas off in a decade. Family and friends stopped inviting me to their celebrations and pastimes as they knew the answer would always be that I was working.

I was charging far below my worth and abilities, working in places that I did not enjoy (the social clubs were a killer – these people actively wait for the act to finish so they can get to the bingo) and I was forfeiting time with my incredible family.

Snatching naps in the car between gigs, sometimes working three jobs in a day to make ends meet, was not how I envisaged spending the rest of my working life.

The kids would cry when I had to leave for work – again. I was on my knees, exhausted, both physically and emotionally.

It was time to start to put together IATQB formally, but I didn't know where to start.

I knew that I had a strong desire to speak, to inspire people and create a movement, but I had no idea how to get on the stage outside of the corporate sector.

There I was, with all of the skills required to help folk but none of the inside knowledge of how to get in front of people and make it work.

I needed to seek out someone who knew more about this kind of thing to guide me.

It was at this very point that Brad Burton came into my life.

Brad Burton, the UK's #1 Motivational Business Speaker, four times author, owner of wildly successful 4Networking and mentor via his private members' club the Now What Club, seemed a pretty decent person to approach for advice.

In the first instance, this may not have been perceived to be a dream match.

There's lots about Brad that I struggled to get to grips with. He is abrasive, brusque and sometimes controversial in the way that he presents himself and with the things that he says.

Brad, of course, knows this and has lots of fun with it.

An exercise that he runs on one of his courses centres around him asking his delegates what people don't like about him. He gleefully receives a barrage of insults, none of which he hasn't heard before and writes them in a column on the whiteboard.

He then asks his delegates to share what people DO like about him and, just as happily, he writes the list on the board.

The lesson comes where he shares that if he were to dilute or take away from himself what people DIDN'T like about him, it would, in turn, dilute what people DID like about him. They were two sides of the same coin, and as such, he would maintain exactly who he was and continue with his mission of trying to make a positive difference in the world without compromising on himself.

The people who he was right for were the people who he would help. The others could go and get what they need elsewhere.

This was a revelation.

I didn't need to be liked by everyone to be a success!

If I was going to have a mentor, I needed someone who knew themselves and was wholly comfortable with who they are. This was one of the things I needed to learn about myself.

I did not need to compromise or change who I was, and I certainly did not need some corporate suit telling me the best way to kiss ass to climb to the top.

I needed someone who had walked a similar path to me and then gone a whole lot further so that I could see what I could be capable of too.

Brad had also come from the council estates in the north of England. He knew hard times in a similar way to me.

Brad and I could have come to blows when I first came across him. I had seen a post of his on social, and it had enraged me.

'You can't trust a fat motivational speaker.'

Brad is often purposefully controversial and polarising on social media to spark debate, but this had me incensed.

How dare this guy call out being fat as being mutually exclusive to being a motivational speaker, the very thing I wanted to be!

In that moment, I made it my mission, as a woman who is both fat AND a powerful speaker, to prove him wrong and I set about doing just that. Not only that, this fucker was going to help me.

I followed him for several months, and as time went on, I started to see Brad, regardless of how he would throw these controversy bombs into my news feed, for the ultimately kind man that he is.

He lifted the people in his circle up. He supported members of his network when they had fallen victim to terminal illness. He was not who I thought he was when I first came across him.

He showed up for his people, warts and all.

Turns out, this was a guy that I could actually get behind.

On the 30th January 2019, I saw a brief video that Brad had posted regarding a personal development event that he was running the very next day called Now What Live. It was a last call for people to attend if they didn't have their tickets. He implored his listeners to get in touch if they were at a crossroads and the only thing stopping them attending was money.

Your girl was at a hell of a crossroads and had about £30 in her bank.

I did not know how much longer I could maintain working at the rate I was. The festive period is one of the busiest times in a performer's calendar and, every year, it would chew me up and spit me out at the end of January unsure of my own name, I would be that exhausted.

All I had was enough petrol to get to the event and a rare day off the next day, so I chanced calling his office, and I spoke to the fabulous Pippa, Brad's co-director, to whom I told my story.

She arranged for me to pay in manageable instalments, and the next day, I found myself in my clapped-out Vauxhall Meriva driving down to Birmingham with no idea what I had just signed up for.

I sat outside Aston Villa football club, and as I did when I was getting ready for most things, I pressed the Live button. I put my makeup on and rallied myself with the help of my amazing Facebook friends (essentially, my fellow Queen Bees at this point) to go into the event in the name of networking and to put myself out there.

Although I received a warm welcome from what was to become, after the event, my very first business family, the Now What Club, I was feeling nervous and out of sorts, so I made my way out of the bustling reception area to an empty seat in the front row in readiness for the event to begin.

It was here that I saw Brad for the first time in real life. I could see he was psyching himself up for his appearance, but I made my way over to him, and I thanked him for helping me find a way to attend, and I told him that we were going to be friends. He still laughs about this because it is not the usual way people introduce themselves to him as he cuts a relatively imposing figure.

Of course, we did become friends, and he agreed to mentor me. I attended all of his training events and invested both time and money in learning what I could from him.

When you first join Brad's mentorship group, you are invited to have a call with him to share what you are working on and what you need help with.

On this call, Brad asked me what my struggles were, and I told him. I was killing myself exchanging time for money with low value, high volume work.

He asked me if I believed that I was excellent at what I do.

Of course, I told him I was.

'Ok, D, fucking charge your worth then. Put your prices up.'

He went on to say, 'Look, it's hard to explain what 'It' is in terms of business or life, but, Kiddo, you have 'It', stop fucking hiding and build the things you want to build.'

'Are your bills paid?' he asked me.

I told him that indeed, my bills were paid... just.

'Right, anything you build from here then is gravy: what the fuck are you waiting for?'

For the first time, someone who had been where I had been and done more than I could imagine, saw me as being capable of doing the same.

This guy was outside of the bucket giving me permission to stop allowing fear to trap me to get the hell out too.

And so the touch paper was lit. There was no going back.

Regardless of how abrasive or controversial he is, underneath this exterior, his drive to help people, to this day, is one of the things I love and respect about him the most.

Since then, Brad has invited me on to his stages, and I achieved what I set out to do when I first came across him and proved I could be a fat motivational speaker.

In Brad's own words, we didn't lock horns; we locked arms.

Mentors can come in many guises.

You do not always have to invest thousands of pounds/dollars in mentorship.

Mentors can be peers, people who you know and trust to give you knowledge and clear guidance delivered to you in a way that you can digest.

They can be educators, teachers whose job it is to deliver a curriculum from which to learn.

They could take the form of a consultant, someone who knows your industry inside out to give you clear direction on strategy.

A mentor could take the form of a coach, just like Heidi did for me at the very beginning. Somebody to ask you the questions that you didn't know to ask yourself and then hold the space for you to come to your own answers.

You may need, as I did when I met our Brad, someone to give you a kick up the arse to stop getting in your own way or to introduce you to people who will be helpful to you.

You can find mentors in books, such as this. It is certainly my pleasure to be doing that very thing for you right now.

When you have decided that you are ready for a mentor, ask yourself – 'What is it that I really need?'

You will find, more often than not, that the following quote will ring true.

> **'When the student is ready, the teacher will appear.'**
>
> **— SIDDHARTHA GUATAMA BUDDHA**

Failing this, identify what you want to learn and go seek out the people that you need.

Join the communities they lead, read their books and go to their events.

If you're feeling particularly drawn to them, you could even reach out directly, introduce yourself, and ask them if they have any mentorship programmes.

Mentors are not Jesus. They are not superior beings to revere and place upon a pedestal.

They are humans. Glorious in both their wisdom and their fallibility. If you require perfection from your role models and mentors, you will be sorely disappointed. Seek out the mentors that show themselves, flaws and all.

You can choose the wisdom to receive.

BORROW THE BELIEF

At the beginning of 2019, having created a small but lovely and loyal online audience, I declared that this year was going to be the 'Year of The Queen Bee'.

We had a hashtag and everything.

The Year of The Queen Bee meant that I was going to throw my whole focus into creating the IATQB business and make it my primary source of income.

I was through missing out on my family and working myself into the ground.

With absolutely no idea how I was going to do this, the decision had been made. I had created my vision board, and I was declaring to the Universe and the world that this was going to go down.

My only strategy was to seek opportunities to talk about my story and plans, then go from there.

This year, I was going to say 'Yes' to every opportunity that would have me speaking to as many people as possible who, in turn, would be sure to see the potential that both I and IATQB had.

It began when I got in the car and drove down to the Now What Live event to meet Brad and, in turn, led me on to a number of courses and events that were absolutely brilliant for meeting more like-minded and driven people.

As I created my Circle of Awesome, I came across more and more epic people, the fabulous Lisa Johnson being one of them.

To put my flag in the ground in terms of my arrival in the personal and business growth industry, I organised an event. A 'coming out to the world', if you will, as a motivational and inspirational speaker.

I had worked hard on creating a series of talks and workshops that I wanted to give some legs to, and I had invited my audience to come along and test some of them out in a live event and celebration of our journey together.

At the event, I was also releasing a merchandise line, and I was seeking models for a photo shoot for my website that day.

It was my intention to find people from diverse backgrounds, who had overcome adversity and created success, to showcase the t-shirts with the IATQB messages of #FLYANYWAY and Show Up, Wise Up, Rise Up.

I knew that if I could get people of influence to support and also witness an IATQB event in action, they would definitely see that I was one to watch and that I wasn't playing around.

Among the people whose work I admired was Lisa Johnson, a passive and semi-passive business strategist whose straight-talking manner and incredible expertise in her field was right up my street.

As someone who had also overcome adversity, in Lisa's case, severe bullying, to go on and create a wildly successful business in the online space, I knew this was a lady I needed in my life.

She was a prime example of success leaving clues, helping women entrepreneurs the world over to create strong and sustainable businesses whereby they didn't have to continually exchange time for money. This was, most definitely, a skill I was lacking.

Seeing as though this was the #YearOfTheQueenBee, I didn't have time to be scared about approaching people to connect. So, I dropped into Lisa's DMs introducing myself, offered her a ticket to my event and asked her to model.

Curious about this strange woman coming from nowhere and offering her tickets to stuff, Lisa, who at the time was in Chicago on business, gave me a call.

I gave her a bit of background, told her about what I was doing and that I was raising money for a local domestic abuse charity as part of my event and that I was excited to know her better.

Sadly, Lisa was unable to make the event but wanted to offer her support. She offered a year's subscription to her epic membership, The GSD Society (it stands for Get Shit Done: I told you this woman was my people) so I offered to send her one of my merch t-shirts instead as a thank you.

We continued to stay in touch and forged a friendship that I value to this day.

When someone knows more than you on a topic, no matter how close you are as friends, it is vital that any exchanges are energetically correct.

Lisa knows how to create businesses that generate serious money using incredible strategies, and it would only be right for me to pay her accordingly for her expertise.

There was, however, a problem.

I did not have the money required to be a part of Lisa's programmes. Hell, I barely had enough money for petrol in my car half the time.

That said, remember, your friendly neighbourhood QB is tenacious. I knew of Lisa's GSD Society, which was, at the time, the most cost-effective way of learning from her, so I forfeited the cost of a bottle of wine a week to join. I would just have to be in her world this way until I had my shit sorted and then invest in what I could when I could.

I absorbed the training in there like a sponge and started to put the foundations together of different packages that I could offer.

In June 2019, Lisa popped a Facebook status up saying that she was going over to Malta for a couple of days in July to get some air miles in and did anyone fancy joining her for an impromptu girls' weekend away.

I just KNEW I had to be there.

I headed straight to the internet to search for flights, certain that I would not be able to afford them (again, my bank account was not in a healthy state). You can imagine both my shock and delight when, by some strange Universal intervention, they were £69 return!

I knew I could hustle up a gig or two to pay for the accommodation a little closer to the time so, with no idea who else would be there, I booked my flight to Malta.

What on the surface of things looked like a bit of a jolly up in the sun, turned out to be a real game-changer for me.

There were about twelve other women that decided to join Lisa in Malta, only one of which I knew. (When I say knew, I mean knew *of*. I was more of a fangirl, sorry, Sam Bearfoot!)

As we have established, your girl is not averse to being uncomfortable, but this trip was wildly out of the realms of what I was used to.

The people going were so far beyond my current state of success that, as I sat in Manchester Airport at 6 am with my Primark hand luggage (I couldn't afford to put a suitcase in the hold, I was that skint), I seriously considered backing out and going home.

These women were multiple five, six and seven-figure earners. Most earned more in a month than I ever had in a year in my corporate roles.

They had the kind of businesses that I could only dream about.

Who the hell did I think I was going over there to hang out with them?

What was I going to bring to any kind of conversation?

My inner Nikki Grahame was having a full-on meltdown, spewing forth tear-streaked venom in the diary room inside my head.

I had to remind myself that, if this was going to be the #YearOfTheQueenBee, I'd best get my ass on that plane and see how the big girls do things.

I had nothing to worry about because from the second I arrived I was welcomed with open arms. In fact, some of these powerhouse women were actually excited to meet me!

The following few days were spent relaxing together, sight-seeing, lunching, laughing and crying together.

I shared my story with them, and they were super generous with their insights and knowledge regarding what I could do to grow my business.

As it turned out, there were many things that I, in turn, was able to offer them too. We often forget, especially when we surround ourselves with people more 'successful' than us, that actually, we may have the skills and expertise that they need too.

When people go to business type retreats, which this inadvertently had become, the best learning and relationships are forged during the breakouts or the downtimes.

This whole long weekend was a break for all of us, so we were all lovely and relaxed, and within that relaxation, we were able to get really creative with our ideas.

Ordinarily, to go on the kind of retreat where these sorts of women would hang out you'd be paying thousands, and here I was, this little unknown fishy in a big pond with about £300 to her name, sharing stories and advice with these absolute jaw-droppers.

What even was my life right now?

I resigned myself to thinking, 'Fuck it, it's been a blast, I've made some wicked connections and some fab memories.' What more could I have asked for? It was a taste of a world that, right now, really wasn't for me, lovely though it was. I just wasn't there yet.

The day before we were due to leave, over a lazy, boozy lunch, the group were asking each other about their plans after the trip.

They each went around the table sharing what they were creating and launching whilst I listened in awe, sipping on my cold pinot grigio, dreading the moment that the conversation would get to me and what I was going to be getting up to.

I did not have a clue.

It inevitably did, and I laughed and told them I had no idea.

Lisa had talked about a mastermind that she was about to launch. It sounded both terrifying and at the same time precisely what I needed, so I nervously laughed and told them 'I have no idea how, but I'm going on Lisa's mastermind. I want to change my life. I want to belong here with you guys and not feel so out of my depth.'

As it stood, I had no idea how to pull the multiple four figure investment out of my arse. Hell, I had barely afforded the couple of hundred quid it had taken me to get to chuffing Malta!

The sun poured through the windows as I looked around the table at these fabulous humans in this beautiful restaurant and felt so small. My eyes welled up. I was so embarrassed.

What happened in the next sixteen and a half minutes changed the course of my business and my life.

The whole group sat forward, and I could see these incredible, caring, sharp as fuck business minds set to work.

Lisa grabbed a pen and a napkin.

'Ok,' she said. 'This can't go on. You are too talented to sit here feeling like this. How much do you want to earn?'

I had never really thought about this properly before because up to this point, I just wanted to earn enough to pay the bills and keep a roof over our heads. There was little extra room for dreams, nor could I envisage an earning capacity beyond the glass ceiling that I had hit in my performing business.

'Errrmmmm... Seven grand,' I said, plucking a figure out of the air.

Completely unperturbed by this, in my mind, astronomical amount of money, Lisa and the girls set about helping me map out something that I could sell.

The group asked me about how, specifically, I could help people. What was the one skill that was my 'zone of genius'?

Having the ability to make people feel good about themselves was not really a monetizable commodity. I would need to get more specific to generate real outcomes for potential clients.

Then it hit me. Teaching people to speak was a no-brainer. I had been helping people of all skill levels take to the stage in all kinds of capacities in my corporate job, and I'd over twenty years honing my own craft in the entertainment industry.

Fear of public speaking is the number one fear in the western world, so was definitely something that many would find themselves blocked with.

In the next quarter of an hour, Lisa gave me a whistle-stop run through of how to launch an online programme, and I lapped it up, furiously scribbling notes, my mind racing at all the things I would need to do to get my shit together.

That said, it didn't sound a million miles away from what I could maybe pull off.

At the very least, I could just give it a bash and see what would pan out for a laugh. After all, my singing was covering the bills so anything that I made here, just like Brad had said earlier in the year, was gravy on top.

Once we had mapped out what I could do, Lisa asked me again, as if to remind herself, 'How much did you want to make again?'

'7k,' I answered. 'But even a couple of hundred quid wouldn't go amiss, I'll take what I can get.'

She laughed.

'Yeah, you might make 7k, Dani, but this will probably make more.'

HA!

What would I even do with more? The thought made me feel a bit sick.

I looked once again around the group, waiting for one of them to crack and let me in on the fact that they were just messing with me.

They didn't.

Sensing my discomfort, one of the women, Kerrie, asked me what was wrong.

I told her that this sort of stuff doesn't happen to people like me.

The group looked at me, aghast.

'Dani, how can you not see what it is that you are capable of? You are sat on gold. You are flipping magnetic. You have the skills and experience to help people. How can you not believe in yourself?'

I didn't know what to say.

I had never been in the company of people who truly saw what it was that I could do and shared that belief with me.

In the past, my potential had scared and intimidated the people around me. It wasn't safe to chase dreams or success, so I continued to play small.

This group of women did not play small. They went out there and claimed the shit out of the things they wanted to achieve.

These women were the embodiment of overcoming adversity to go on to create lives of their own design.

And they believed in *me*.

'If you can't believe in yourself right now,' Kerrie continued, 'you can just borrow our belief in you until you prove us right.'

I came away from that trip with a whole new plan, friends for life and a deeper understanding of myself.

I was going to make this happen. Even if the belief was borrowed, for now, I was taking it and running as fast as I could.

The launch made £16,000 and the programme we created that day has become my signature programme Bee Heard which, so far, has seen hundreds of business owners smash through their own limiting beliefs and sharing their stories on stage.

It's a trip that I will never forget and for which I will be forever grateful.

I want you to think of all the things you really want. Imagine what you could be capable of if only you believed it.

And if you're struggling to have that belief yourself, here, you can borrow some of mine.

WHAT CONFIDENCE REALLY IS

'You're a performer, Dani; you must be super confident.'

This a common misconception about me, or rather, it was until I learned more about myself and accepted who I truly am in more recent years.

In this chapter, I want to explore with you some different personality types and then have a delve into what real confidence actually is.

The reason I want to explore this with you is that there are a number of expectations around personality types, and while they are handy to help get the gist of someone, they never really give us the full picture.

These personality types and true confidence are not mutually exclusive.

Let's take a look.

Being a performer by nature means I will often reside in an extroverted state.

As such, people will comment on how confident I *must* be.

This is a funny old conundrum for lots of extroverts out there.

If we look at the traits of the extrovert, we find that, according to the 'rules', they tend to: –

- Like to be the centre of attention
- Energetically recharge by being in other people's company
- Prefer to communicate by talking
- Have a wide circle of connections and acquaintances
- Feel isolated and listless after spending too long on their own

However, extroversion has several drawbacks, such as: –

-They can be perceived as being disingenuous or fake.

- They can feel under pressure to be 'switched on' all the time, leaving little space to relax

- They may rely on external feedback for validation

Just because an extrovert gains their energy externally, this does not mean that they are exempt from feeling a lack of confidence.

Introverts, on the other hand, according to the same set of rules, tend to: –

- Prefer writing over talking
- Enjoy and seek out solitude to energetically recharge
- Be described as quiet
- Will watch and process situations and information before making decisions
- Be very self-aware

As with extroversion, introversion does not come without its own set of problems.

- They may struggle to grow their networks
- They may miss out on opportunities due to declining invitations to events outside of their comfort zone
- They may get overlooked or overshadowed
- They may be seen as standoffish or unapproachable

All of this does not mean, just as with extroverts not being exempt from feeling a lack of confidence, that introverts cannot be confident human beings. Far from it. There is much power in THE quiet and rock-solid confidence that our glorious introverts can exude.

As a child, the way I sought validation was through acceptance from those around me.

I was the loud, annoying kid because I wanted to be seen and feel significant. This need, because our family was so busy, wasn't met as well as I required. This does not make for a confident child, nor does it make for a confident grown-up.

I would wear the mask of what the perception of confidence was, but I did not actually feel it properly for many years.

Personality profiling within the workplace is commonplace and a great tool to use when recruiting and building teams.

The problem with this is that we find it easy to pigeon-hole ourselves and those around us when we are privy to this information.

Take the Quadrant Theory.

There are a butt tonne of personality profiling systems and tools out there, many of them fabulous. Aside from introversion and extroversion, as we've already discussed, most of them boil down to the following concept.

There are four main personality types.

1 – Results Driven

These are goal-oriented people who are concerned with results.

They are more likely to take charge in group situations.

They make quick decisions.

They are strong-willed, determined and may be competitive.

2 – Details Driven

Details driven people are analytical by nature.

They will ask lots of questions before committing to a course of action.

They are cautious, precise and deliberate in their actions.

They will be more likely to act if the payoff is clear to them.

3 – People Driven

This personality type will seek harmony and inclusion for all involved in a project.

They will support others.

They create trust in group situations.

They are patient and relaxed.

4 – Idea Driven

These are sociable and dynamic creatures.

They are great at creating excitement and drumming up support.

They are demonstrative and enthusiastic.

They are great persuaders.

Just as with introverts and extroverts, all these personality types have their own set of positives and negatives, and it is here that I find that things get sticky.

It is very easy to either completely resign yourself to your personality type and become inflexible, leaving you little room for growth. Also, it is challenging to shake others' perceptions of the negative aspects of these, once they are known.

It will be of no surprise to you that I fell firmly into the last category on the quadrant.

I am indeed one of life's fire-starters. I love nothing more than getting people excited about things, from events to their own abilities.

The downfall to this is that I would struggle to finish the things that I started or I could be impulsive or disorganised. Probably one of the hardest things about fitting this personality type was that, within the workplace, I found it hard to be taken, or even take myself, seriously.

I was not granting myself the acceptance of the knowledge that while, yes, in my most relaxed and natural state, I would lead with this personality type, I was still highly capable of 'swapping hats' so to speak.

Just because you lead with a particular behaviour type does not mean you are incapable of calling in the other types.

The more I learned about myself, and as I grew and changed (as everyone does), I found that I became more results-focused and goal-driven.

When I became a parent, a whole new side of my personality started to grow, and I found myself sitting within Type Three a lot more.

All this is to say, my Loves, is that it is truly wonderful to know these things about yourself, to get a baseline understanding. It is far more important, however, to accept that you get to call in these traits as you require them, like superpowers.

This is not confidence.

Confidence is a whole other beast.

Now we have established what confidence isn't, let's have a nosy at what this elusive feeling is, then.

Confidence, or lack thereof, is the slayer of many people's dreams.

I hear this all the time.

'I could never go to a networking group.'

'I could never get on stage and speak about what I do.'

'I couldn't possibly go for that job.'

It's all the bullshit we tell ourselves when we are scared.

Lack of confidence has ball all to do with your personality type or whether you are an introvert or extrovert.

Lack of confidence is <u>fear</u>.

Here are some things you can do to get out of your own damn way and get to grips with unleashing a more confident you.

1. Take small steps that scare you and build up your resistance to them. Every time you survive a step, celebrate! You didn't die; you have 100% survival rate; now go again!

2. Own your whole self in all of its gloriousness and imperfection.

3. Know that you are valid, whatever personality type you are. We need all of them, especially yours. You are unique, and you are necessary.

4. Know, please know, that everyone is winging it. The more and more 'successful' people I come across, the more I know this to be true.

5. Find reasons to be grateful – fear cannot live alongside gratitude.

6. Speaking of gratitude, swap out apologising all the time by expressing thanks. This fills your conversations with appreciation and makes both sides feel good. For example, instead of saying, 'I'm sorry for babbling on,' when you have taken longer than you would have liked to explain something, say, 'Thank you for listening.' Or instead of 'Sorry, I'm late,' Try, 'Thank you for waiting for me.'

7. Embody confidence. When you hold your body, consciously, in a decisive manner – standing up straight, broadening and relaxing your shoulders and planting your feet firmly on the ground, for example, the limbic part of your brain (the part of your brain that responds to emotion, not language) will register that you are holding a strong position and will

respond accordingly by not firing off as much of the stress hormones adrenalin and cortisol. Instead, it will release the alpha hormone, testosterone, and this will have you feeling unstoppable.

Above all, confidence is that quiet knowing and acceptance of **exactly** who you are.

And who you are is fucking glorious.

ON SWEARING

> **"This is Big Brother, do not say 'Fuck' or 'Bugger'"**
>
> — **LEIGH FRANCIS**

You MAY HAVE NOTICED that I get a little sweary when I get excited.

The word 'shit' appears approximately 4345 times[1] in this book alone and to quote another Queen Bee, Beyonce – 'I ain't sorry.'

In my house, as long as swearing isn't AT someone, isn't done in anger and is in context, then I'm pretty easy going about it.

I know everyone has different opinions on this, but I honestly believe that there are worse words out there than 'fuck' or 'bugger'.

I genuinely believe that words like 'hate' and calling people names like 'Stupid' is far more damaging and as such, this kind of verbal venom receives more of a reprimand over here at Casa del Wallace.

'What on earth does swearing have to do with becoming the Queen Bee and this flying anyway malarkey?' I hear you cry!

This chapter is an extension of the previous. I want us to start relinquishing any designs we had on perfection and start to own our shit.

Industry and societal standards are constructs.

Some make perfect sense and are there to keep us safe, for example, don't go round killing each other or stealing from your nan, etc. Some are just to keep you conforming and to keep those around you comfortable. The fun bit is that we do not have to follow the latter: those we can play with.

If you cast your mind all the way back to Chapter 1, I would like to remind you that this book is not about being comfortable. It's about being YOU. It's about revelling in your fabulous, messy, wonderful, unflinching you-ness.

Perfection is a lie. It can get right in the bin.

These perfectly curated instafabulous influencers, the laptop lifestylers and the media want to sell you something.

What you must keep in mind is that, regardless of what they are selling, be it the latest MUST HAVE hair products or the ridiculous skinny teas that make you shit yourself, the aim is to make you feel crappy and not enough so that you buy their products in the sure and certain hope that you will be a better, more fulfilled person.

It's bollocks.

Happiness and fulfilment come from falling so hard in love with yourself and your life, that none of that shit matters any more.

Don't get me wrong, I'm not saying don't buy the hair stuff or the diarrhoea tea (ok, maybe don't do that), but when you see the ads or these perfect posts, please stop comparing yourself to whatever version of perfection you are being served and think about why you are seeing this stuff.

It's not real.

You are so much more than this, and you have more to give the world.

Your journey to being this awesomely epic version of yourself begins with getting to know yourself all over again.

When I was in employment, I was lucky enough to have some kick-ass jobs; some would have said I was a 'high-flyer'.

Being a high-flyer meant that I had to dress a certain way, talk a certain way and act a certain way.

When I began building my own businesses, I swore to myself (pardon the pun) that, as much as was legal, kind and in alignment with my values and morals, I would no longer subscribe to restricting myself in such a way.

If I wanted visible tattoos, I would flipping well have them. In fact, as soon as I decided that this was going to form part of my 'look', I went straight to one of my favourite tattoo artists and ceremoniously had some 'job-stoppers', my hand tattoos in this instance, done.

If I didn't want to wear makeup one day, then I wouldn't.

If I wanted to wear a cheerleader outfit to work (it has been known) then I would be there, pom-poms akimbo.

Once I had decided that I was going to be genuinely, unapologetically, ridiculously me, magic started to happen in my life and business.

I was free to explore what worked and didn't work for me and, as a result, became more and more comfortable and accepting of myself.

I began to dig on the head-scarfed, tattooed, honest, fiercely kind, loyal, if a little sweary, Dani and it was from there that people started to take notice.

People buy from people and the more real you show up, the easier it is to know, like and trust you.

You don't need to *convince* people to like you.

It is worth acknowledging, at this point, that in doing this, you will switch some people off.

AND THAT IS OK.

This was something that I struggled to get to grips with at first.

My desperate need to be validated externally and liked by as many people as possible meant that the concept that, shock/horror, there may be people out there that may not like me, filled me with fear.

I mean, I'm a kind person, I do my best to do everything with the best and most honest of intentions, I'm funny as shit. What's not to love?

But, to quote the fabulous Dita Von Teese –

 "You can be the ripest, juiciest peach in the world, and there's still going to be somebody who hates peaches."

There are 7.5 billion people in the world; it would be ludicrous to think that every single person was going to dig on me, no matter how hard I tried.

In fact, by even attempting this, I would end up trying to be all things to everyone and then diluting who I truly wanted to be.

Confused people don't buy, and if I didn't know who I was and what I stood for, how would the people I wanted to attract know I was safe?

Things like allyship, diversity, kindness, tolerance and a lack of fear when discussing difficult topics all became the things I wanted to hang my hat on and that is not for everyone, regardless of how much I would like it to be.

It became clear to me that I would need to repel some people in order to attract the people I truly wanted in my world.

I went from being scared of turning people off to being happy when someone unsubscribed from my mailing list, left my group or unfollowed me. This simply meant they didn't like the veritable peach that I am and so by removing themselves, they made space for people who did.

You will attract the right people to you, YOUR people, by being totally uncompromising with who you are and how you show up.

Whether you choose to swear or not, that's your bag. It's all optional.

You do you, Boo.

---

1. This is a slight exaggeration

SELF-CARE

I'M GOING to call this now.

Out of all of the chapters in this book, THIS one, if you get this right for yourself, will be a game-changer and, potentially, the catalyst for everything else you would like to happen in your life to fall into place.

Remember when we were talking about shit shoes earlier in the book? Well, we are going to delve a little deeper into what that means for you in a holistic sense because it really is so flipping important.

This book is about eradicating self-sabotage so that you can #FlyAnyway, and this is an impossibility if you do not make yourself a priority. The crazy thing is that this is a hugely alien concept to many of us, especially for those of the female persuasion.

Women and those who identify more within their femininity will frequently find themselves to be the carers and the nurturers of those around them.

I would hazard to guess that, although the readers of this book will be a whole spectrum of genders, our fabulous womenfolk will fall foul of the following in larger numbers.

Are you the last to look after yourself?

Are you giving so much time and energy to others and left with very little for you?

Are you feeling stressed out or overwhelmed?

Do you find it difficult to express your needs or even bloody well identify what they are so that you can?

Take a breath with me and let's get to grips with this.

For the dudes and the more masculine amongst us, this does not mean to say that self-care is not for you, so pop yer pitchforks down, you just tend to be better at this than us feminine folk.

A prime example of this is my husband.

At the beginning of our relationship, I wondered if there was some sort of gastric health issue going on with him because, seriously, it takes the guy about 45 minutes to take a crap.

FORTY. FIVE. FUCKING. MINUTES.

The whole idea of spending that long on the loo had always been beyond me.

Prior to meeting Wallace (yes, I call him by his surname, it's a thing), I was a single mum of two under-threes. Going to the toilet was a smash-and-grab affair that did not involve closed doors or, in many instances, personal space.

It was the same for showering or, indeed, any personal care I attempted.

It wasn't safe, of course, to leave the toddlers completely unattended whilst I took care of business so I just accepted that I had to get in and out of there as quickly as I possibly could with them close by to make sure that they were ok.

When Wallace eventually moved in with us, I would get infuriated that he would disappear for what seemed like half the bloody day when he needed to poop until I realised what it was that he was actually, albeit subconsciously, doing.

He was taking some time for himself.

He would take his phone or read a book or magazine whilst he was in there and just... 'have a sit', as he would say.

Not only this, but he would also, can you believe... lock the door!

This guy had the audacity to just go and take some time for himself when the mood took him.

My mind was blown.

I did not know this was something a person could do!

The real revelation came when I realised that now things were much more stable in terms of having an extra set of eyes and ears in the house, there was absolutely no reason for me not to do the same.

I had gotten so used to having to do everything quickly that it had become a habit, and not a very healthy one at that, so instead of being resentful about how long my husband took to look after himself, as it were, I started to do the same.

I still haven't gotten my head around sitting on the toilet for the best part of an hour, but my shower time and other time spent on my self-care became more of a non-negotiable and boy, do I feel better for it.

Self-care is a funny old business.

It has become quite the buzz term in more recent times and is often regarded by those who are loath to practise it, as they do not make themselves a priority, as selfish.

Please hear me, my darling reader, when I tell you that it is quite the opposite.

You will have heard the term, 'You cannot pour from an empty cup,' or have been reminded of the fact that when you are in a plane, should the oxygen masks come down, you should always put your own on first.

Clichés are based on truth, my loves.

You are no good to anyone and, more importantly, yourself if you are not looking after *you*.

The world needs you strong, both emotionally and physically, if you are to make a difference to it.

I thought it might be helpful to have a look at some of the best self-care strategies to get you looking after yourself again, if this is an area that has been compromised.

In the mainstream media, we get told self-care is about candles and bubble baths or going to the hairdressers or a spa.

Magazines bombard us with what they think we should be doing to 'look after' ourselves, but what about those of us, myself included, that HATE baths? What about those of us that would rather watch our parents go at it than sit in a hairdresser making small talk about holidays?

Before we start, I want to make it super clear that self-care is not a 'one size fits all' situation.

It is different for *everyone*.

I implore you to try out any and all of the ways to look after yourself to see what works for you.

What I share with you here is a non-exhaustive list.

Ok, so let's get our head around a bit of theory.

The Emotional Bank Account.

This concept runs on the premise that your energy and emotions run like a balance sheet.

If you are giving your time and energy to something, to create balance you need to do something to replace it.

This could look like resting, meditating, doing something you enjoy or hanging out with people that have energy that you dig.

If you're out of balance, you will find yourself feeling stressed, exhausted, susceptible to burnout and physical or mental illness OR so self-indulged you get nothing done, and you don't grow.

There are so many different kinds of self-care and ways to practise it.

Here are a few –

Physical

We go to the doctors to seek help when things are not going well with our bodies, but if we spent more time looking after our bodies on a more consistent basis, we would need this in a much-reduced capacity.

Nourishing ourselves with good food and moving it are two of the most essential things we can do to look after ourselves.

How we move, how often we move and what we fuel our bodies with has a direct impact on our energy levels, stress levels and therefore our success levels.

What I am not saying here is that we should all be going on a super crazy diet and running marathons, y'all: I don't even run for a bus, but we would feel and do better by being more mindful about how we treat our incredible bods.

When my mental health took a hit in the past, simple physical self-care such as showering and teeth brushing could become seemingly impossible tasks, but when I did them, I felt better—every time.

Physical self-care doesn't need to be complicated. Keeping ourselves clean and fed are acts of love for ourselves and should be treated accordingly.

Our bodies are our only real home for the whole of our lives. How we look after them will determine the length of our stay.

Emotional

Learning how to navigate our emotions and understanding ourselves as best we can are the key to being able to rock and roll our way through life like a star.

Learning how to tap into your intuition, and seeking emotional balance, allows you to react to all manner of situations as they unfold in a way that is safe. It also helps you maintain control over most outcomes in most situations.

Contrary to what we would like to believe, there are no negative emotions, even the ones that we don't enjoy so much, like sadness or anger.

Our emotions are all there to help keep us safe, and the more we get in tune with them, the better we can deal with life.

Allowing yourself the knowledge that your feelings are totally valid as you are feeling them, whatever it is that you are feeling, is hugely freeing.

It is a massive misconception that you need to maintain positivity at all times. The PMA Police can bugger right off.

Sometimes situations are shitty, and you can feel shitty about them.

To pretend any other way can create what is called 'cognitive dissonance' whereby you actually make yourself feel *worse* by thinking you 'should' be feeling differently.

Stop shafting yourself with a Should Stick and lean into how you are feeling. Allow it and learn coping mechanisms and tools to help you work with them.

Learning how to navigate your feelings is different from trying to micro-manage them. Give yourself a break.

Professional

Professional self-care is often much lower down on the list, but it is just as important as the rest.

Most of us spend a third of our lives at work—a whole third.

With this in mind, it would make sense to find ways to make sure that we are looking after ourselves whilst we are there, right?

Right.

I'm going to cover some of the things you can get more mindful of in your professional life:

Managing Your Time – This could look like making sure you only check your emails at specific times in the day and ensuring you have strict response periods for these emails.

The snag with not doing this is that you can get bogged down in the to-ing and fro-ing of emails and not get to do the things you need to get done.

Boundaries – This is always a fun one and one that I struggled with in previous years.

People will treat you with the respect and the value with which you treat yourself. With boundaries, you get to set the bar around how and when to expect to work or to allow people to have contact with you.

But this does not always come naturally to us. Setting boundaries means that you need to put your needs right to the top of the list to keep you productive.

Common reasons that you may find that people do not respect your boundaries are –

You may allow too much flexibility, and are contactable around the clock, then wonder why people expect you to be available to them all the time.

You don't tell people what your boundaries are and are shocked when they push past them.

You apologise for setting boundaries like you don't even want them.

You don't hold others accountable for their actions or their promises to you.

We need to remember; our values and expectations are not the same as everyone else's, so it is imperative that we are clear with what is acceptable for us and what isn't. This kind of boundary setting will apply to social self-care too.

Saying No or Turning Away Work – Again, especially at the beginning, I would find it difficult turning away work for fear that the work may dry up.

This comes from a lack mentality. It wasn't so long ago that I was homeless and fighting to pay even the most basic of bills and I was scared shitless.

I ended up taking people who were not ready to work with me and gigs that were low paying and soul-destroying.

When you do this, it is very difficult to enjoy what you are doing and if we spend a third of our life at work, ain't nobody got time for that.

The thing is, if you have robust systems, a solid ideal client profile, kick-ass offerings and awesome strategies in place, there is no reason for the work to dry up.

I was guilty of all of the above in vain attempts to people-please, but this left me exhausted and resentful.

Getting to grips with your professional self-care makes space for you to be happy and productive in your work life, which in turn will help you lead a happy and healthy home life.

Social

There is a lot of learning around our social self-care that we can apply from the previous Professional section of this chapter, but there are other things you can put in place from a social self-care perspective that will be mega helpful for you too.

Support networks are a great place to start.

Having people on which you can rely, not just when the going gets tough but when the going is good, is an epic strategy that you can implement.

Just like when we spoke about those pesky crabs earlier in the book, have people around you who don't bring you down and, instead, lift you up.

Knowing how you build up your energy is helpful here too. If you are an extrovert, make sure you create time to be around the folk who make you happy. Conversely, for you introverts, don't feel guilty for excusing yourself when you have had your fill in social situations.

Financial

Finances are a huge source of stress for many, and it is common for us to hide from our financial well-being.

After I lost the house, it took me years to even consider looking at my credit report. I just assumed that it was never going to right itself and that I could never apply for credit ever again.

The weight of the shame I was carrying, mixed with the generational belief that money had to be hard-won in order for it to be worth having, wore heavy.

I buried my head in the sand, and it will be no surprise to you that my finances did not magically right themselves. SHOCKER.

It would need me to heal my relationship with money and face my fears. I needed to take a look at what was going on to fix the situation.

Sometimes, self-care looks like doing things that make you uncomfortable in the short-term to help make you successful beyond your wildest dreams in the long-term.

If money is your sticking point, bring in a financial advisor or a money coach to help you get clear and set yourself some goals.

You can only fix the things you know about.

Look after your money, and it will look after you. Love it, and it will love you back.

Environment

When Wallace and I got married, I actually wrote into my vows that, although I would work hard for our family, I was not to be expected to do the housework.

It just doesn't work for me. I'm a big picture thinker with lots of stuff to get done. This QB has designs on world domination, and I categorically do not want to spend my time doing ridiculous things like cleaning or even worse... ironing!

The only issue with this is that with three kids, two dogs plus the two of us, the house, much to my dismay, does not keep itself.

As an aside from this, just as with my personal self-care, my environmental self-care would take a huge hit when I was feeling unwell, and tasks like the household chores would become impossible or so out of hand that I wouldn't even know where to start.

It is here that I decided that, although I would not contribute physically to this absolute household necessity, I would do what I was able to help.

I got a cleaner.

If I could pinpoint the single biggest kindness that I have ever paid myself, the most impactful act of self-care, getting a cleaner to come help with the house is top of the list, hands down.

I could snog them when they come around once a week to do the things that I find myself too busy or overwhelmed to do.

There was a fair bit of shame around this area too: would people think I'm lazy?

Would it make me a middle-class wanker?

In reality, anyone who knows me knows that I am the furthest away from lazy that a human being could be and, as for being a middle-class wanker...actually, in fairness, I have developed a rather meaningful relationship with avocado toast in the last couple of years so that may be but swings and roundabouts, eh?

Your environment, whether it's your workspace or your living space, really does affect the energy you will have when you are in them.

Tidy house, tidy mind and all that.

Spiritual

Knowing what is important to you and connecting with that regularly is so important as you will make life choices informed by these every day of your life.

Disconnection with your core values and beliefs leads to resentment and also can leave you feeling anxious and stressed.

Making sure you check in with your moral compass when it comes to life choices is essential to keeping your path aligned and stress away from the door.

Another game-changer for me was meditation.

Allowing my busy mind to settle so that I could sort through how I felt about things as a voyeur to my thoughts instead of an active participant has been transformational.

The interesting thing here, perhaps, is that the method of meditation that works for me is a little different to the serene, cross-legged, eyes closed variety, although I have learned how to practise this and it is super helpful.

Meditation looks, in my case, like putting time aside to put my makeup on. It's like those grown-up mindfulness colouring books you can get but on my face. I am forced to concentrate on just one thing at a time and it allows me to get present and in the moment. It is especially helpful when my mind is buzzing with the fifty fafillion ideas I have every day.

Another method of meditation (I have since found out this is called 'Conscious Meditation') is driving.

When I was singing more regularly, I spent A LOT of time in the car. I would listen to podcasts and audiobooks, but most of the time, I hatched my best plans whilst driving. My conscious thoughts were on the road and in the act of driving, but my mind would drift, and all manner of awesome would pop up.

There are lots of ways to meditate, and I cannot recommend making mindfulness a part of your daily practice highly enough.

Spoon Theory – How to manage when things go wrong

What about when the balance has been tipped in the wrong direction for too long, and you begin to struggle?

Mental health is just as important as physical health but, because of the more subtle ways that poor mental health shows itself, it can be hard to pinpoint when you may need help.

This happens more and more, especially as we live in times that are changing faster than some of us can keep up with.

I make no secret about my personal battles with my mental health. When things get particularly bad, I have to hunker down and take note of what I'm doing to help myself.

I would get so overwhelmed by life and all the things I needed to do, and I did not have all of the strategies that we have discussed so far in this chapter in place, so I would become ill.

I was riddled with anxiety that would, in turn, dress itself up as depression because I was so exhausted from living emotionally and psychologically on the edge.

Here's a way of thinking that helped me get things back in order.

The idea is this. When you wake up in the morning, you have a number of energy units: let's call them spoons.

When you are struggling with your mental health, imagine that at the start of every day you are given a finite number of the spoons, let's say twelve.

Each activity you do will take away a certain number of spoons.

For example -

Get out of bed = 1 spoon

Have a shower = 2 spoons

Do the food shopping = 4 spoons

And so on.

Use them up too quickly, and it could leave you depleted and exhausted.

Self-care, if you're at this point, could be saying NO to something so you can rest and replenish your spoon supply. Rest is crucial here.

It could be celebrating the fact that you have completed small wins that have led to your survival that day. No victory is too small when you feel like this.

Work out what works for you. Rid yourself of this guilt we place upon ourselves for looking after ourselves.

Your success and your health depend on it.

Recovery is JUST as important as intensity.

If you need any help at all or feel like you are struggling with your mental health, head on over to the back of the book where I've popped you some useful links to help you should you need.

Look after yourselves, my loves. You are important.

You need to be strong so that you can fly.

CHUFTY BADGES

Despite being such a tiny set of islands, the United Kingdom has the widest variety of local accents and dialects per square mile than most other places in the world.

Being a lover of language and, of course, being a speaker and speaker coach, it fascinates me how people speak and the phrases they use.

I'm from the north of England, and this comes with its own set of sayings and words that are equal parts funny and endearing.

From 'Seeing your arse' when you get annoyed to 'putting the wood in t' hole' to close a door, northern England is a lush and fertile land of fabulous phrases.

One of my all-time favourites is the sarcastic use of the term 'Chufty Badge'.

The term 'chuffed' means to be pleased with oneself, and a 'Chufty Badge' is a fictitious award for doing something that you really should have done anyway or something that doesn't take much effort.

One may be awarded for bragging about something that is considered easy.

The acerbic northern wit may be an acquired taste, but there is no harm or malice intended. Typically, these little digs are said in jest, and everyone is in on the joke.

It's a relatively old saying but fun nevertheless and I, for one, am campaigning for a revival.

For example, you may have hung a coat up and then told someone what you just did. That person may say, 'What do you want? A Chufty Badge?'

What is really being asked here is - 'What kind of recognition do you want when you should be doing this anyway?'

This term got me thinking about how we reward ourselves in business, especially if you are an entrepreneur.

When I ran or was part of a team in the corporate world, performance was often driven in the form of incentives or competitions. Prizes would vary from fabulous weekends away to pizzas delivered to the office.

We would laugh at the variety of prizes and joke that actually it didn't matter what prizes were on the table; it was the recognition that was important and that lit the fire in our bellies. To coin another northern phrase, 'In competition, people will do owt for an Oxo cube.'

Multi-millionaire, best-selling author, world-class speaker and coach Tony Robbins talks of the six basic human needs – Certainty, Uncertainty, Growth, Contribution, Connection and Significance.

Incentivising work or the completion of tasks in this way really does tick the boxes of our needs requirements.

This is difficult to do when you work for yourself or when there is no one around to recognise your work.

If well respected global marketeers like Lee Odden maintain that,

 'People will work for a living but die for recognition,'

how in the world do we fulfil those needs in our work and home lives?

No one is really giving out Chufty Badges, right?

Part of stepping up into our powerful bad-ass, best versions of ourselves takes us being able to recognise *ourselves* for our achievements and wins, even when no-one is looking.

There are several ways you can do this, both large and small.

Creating feelings of joy in what we do will anchor us and spur us on to the next achievement. If you go a long time without any kind of celebration or reward, it will become very easy to lose motivation and sight of why you're even doing what you're doing in the first place.

By positively reinforcing your wins, you will lock that feeling in, and you will be more likely to hit that next level.

Reward assists momentum.

So, what can you do to reward yourself when you need to fill that recognition cup up?

Here is a list of suggestions that I gathered from some of the Queen Bees in my IATQB Community to get you started!

> ❝ *'I learned something from Tony Robbins that's become part of my mantra. I high-five myself. I've come up with my own version of a Wonder Woman pose, and I have a theme song. Its sounds a bit like the Rocky Theme song.'*
>
> — KATHERINE ANN BYAM

'Vino, chocolate and a big bag of Flamin' Hot Wotsits!'

— LISA JANE

Now that I have finally started my career and I'm earning more money, I try to treat myself to things more often. I book to stay somewhere or do something fun! Shows, waterparks, hotel getaways. And if all else fails... additional sleep!

— REBECCA POLLARD

'I always make myself a brew, and I write down the win in a journal. It may seem silly, but I close my eyes for a moment, and I remember a time when there were not many wins, and I like to think that sends a beam of gratitude out to acknowledge the difference from then to now. I also have been allowing myself "guilty pleasure" hours or days depending on the win.'

— DAWNI BETH BAXTER

'*A new subscription box. This month's was Barry's Cactus Club. I currently have the following subscription boxes as rewards to myself: Cactus Club, a razor club, a gluten-free snack club, a knickers club... I love post, and this makes me happy!*'

— ALICE DRURY

'*I like to set myself goals that are stretching but also achievable. When I get it right, and it all just happens as it should, there will be a celebratory drink and meal with hubby whilst listening to music we love and sometimes a little music jam with hubby playing the guitar and me singing.*'

— SONAL DAVE

'*Dancing to Northern Soul in my knickers, seriously big knickers!*'

— JO WILSON

> 'A slogan tee, a new lippy or something pretty that's just for me. Failing that it's gin, dark chocolate and an early night! #rocknroll!'

— EMMA ROSCOE

> 'I treat myself to something shiny for me, and then I book something nice to do with the people I love, whilst wearing said sparkly gift. Time is so very precious, the greatest gift of all.'

— LIZ STEPHENSON

As you can see, rewards can come in all shapes, sizes and levels of expense. What is most important is that you choose rewards for yourself that genuinely make you feel good!

Get your to-do list out and make sure you have some rewards lined up ready for when you tick stuff off!

Make sure you tag me in your Chufty Badge moments so I can celebrate with you!

CLOSED MOUTHS DON'T GET FED

THIS CHAPTER actually contains a few excerpts from my very first mini-book of the same name. I swear I'm not being lazy. It totally fits here, and I promise you that this is absolutely relevant to this point in our journey together.

When presenting yourself to the world as the total rock-star kind of royalty that you are, you gotta get comfortable telling people about yourself.

Glossophobia - the fear of public speaking is the number one fear in the western world. I was gobsmacked when I learned this as it was something that I had been doing since I was about twelve or thirteen years old!

So many people that I come across have done themselves out of opportunities because they have been afraid to speak up and share what it is that they are good at.

It made me so sad to see talented people miss out on all of the glorious abundance that is their birthright because they were scared.

This is precisely the reason I developed a large facet of IATQB around helping business owners share their business and mission message. I now help thousands of people all over the world tap into their story and the reasons why they do what they do so that they can reach more of their ideal people and, of course, make more money in the process.

It was a no brainer for me. With over twenty years on stage and fifteen in the corporate training room and boardroom, this was, without a doubt, my calling when it came to helping people truly #FlyAnyway.

In this chapter, I want to help you get thinking about how you can use your voice to elevate yourself, be it in life or business.

It's worthwhile remembering that public speaking occurs *whenever* you are talking to a group of people. This doesn't just happen on big stages in front of hundreds of people.

It could be in the form of a small group presentation, a sales pitch or a team meeting.

It could be when you are at the PTA meetings for school, and you want to share something with the other parents.

There are so many scenarios in which you could find yourself with an opportunity to speak.

The world has a habit of changing rapidly, now more than ever. It is up to us as entrepreneurs, thought leaders, change-makers and home-creators to keep a finger on the pulse of what's happening in terms of human and business behaviour.

Forty or fifty years ago, most business was done in real life or over the phone. Networking often involved small community/local network events run by groups such as the local Chamber of Commerce. Alternatively, if you wanted to access business further afield, lots of travel would be required. As such, companies were made and broken on the owner's ability or capacity to travel OR their ability to garner support within the local community.

Then came the rise of the internet and travel became less of a necessity. Video calling and online networking became 'the' way to grow a business.

It was then we saw the rise of the Online Entrepreneur.

This has, no doubt, been a fruitful time for those savvy enough to keep up to date with technology, BUT this new decade is seeing a shift once more.

Trends are showing that consumers and business owners alike, whilst often making their initial connections online, are showing more and more of an interest in taking those connections and forging deeper, more meaningful relationships offline and out in the real world, especially in the weeks and months after a global pandemic. Folks are craving ways to better connect.

We are seeing more live eventing and networking opportunities coming through and this is a great place to get yourself seen and heard.

Live videos and stories on social media platforms are also on the increase. If you are not using this channel of marketing for your business, you are leaving money on the table. It is the quickest way to get in front of your ideal clients.

Speaking provides you with the ability to get your message heard in a 'one to many' capacity.

Here are some reasons why you most definitely should be speaking: -

Expert Positioning

When you stand to speak, you automatically position yourself as an expert on the topic you are talking about. The people in your audience immediately look to you as a source of information. By having talks and topics prepared and being unafraid to speak, you are allowing yourself to be seen and heard. The more you are seen and heard, the more likely it is people will remember you, and when they need you, you will be the person they call upon.

Speeding Up the Know/Like/Trust Process

Consumers/clients do not make purchases or investments if they do not know, like or trust a brand. It takes on average between seven to ten exposures to a product or service for them to decide to buy. This process is accelerated when you have a relationship with your consumer. The easiest and quickest way to do that is by speaking with them or to them.

Turbo Charging Your Network

You will hear me say this all the time. Your Network Is Your Net Worth. This is so important that I have written you a whole chapter about this. By speaking, you will be connecting with more people. This does not just mean clients, but also people of influence and potential collaborators.

Collaborations are magical things in that contributing parties not only get to work with aligned brands, but you give and get access to each other's network and audiences.

Sometimes speaking doesn't have to result in a sale. It could have you meet like minds who you can add to your tribe of power sisters/brothers/siblings. THAT is worth its weight in gold.

Improve Your Confidence

Often, people say to me, 'I don't have the confidence to speak.' They will tell me that they need confidence first, and then they will speak. They want to wait until they feel confident.

Oh, hell no.

I want to challenge this belief and tell you that actually, you can grow your confidence *by* speaking. The more you do, the better you will get. It's the same with anything, my lovely friend. You will never be as inexperienced as the first time you do something, and to get experience, you need to bloody well do it! The sense of satisfaction and achievement you will get by going for it is REAL! I will talk later on in the book about how you can trick your brain into banishing those fears and have you striding out on stage like the royalty you are.

In short, speaking is the BEST way to get yourself noticed, positioned and most importantly converting if it is within the field of business that you want to get further.

Closed mouths don't get fed.

I was on the BBC's 'The Voice' circa 2014/2015.

Don't get excited... blink, and you miss me.

I had been scouted in local auditions and went through the whole process of further auditions, screen tests and rehearsals until it came to filming at Media City in Salford.

Y'all. Right then, right there, was my big break. My fifteen minutes of fame.

I had been taking a run-up my whole life to this point. As a singer for all these years, many an audience member/family member/friend had told me that this is where I should be. The age of reality telly had conditioned me to think that there was no other way for a girl like me.

So, there I was, Media City, Salford, for three days of filming all sorts of stuff before the big show. Interviews, pieces to cameras, producers WILLING me to cry when I was sharing my story. Nervous entrants all in a holding area. The director paced me up and down the corridor just before I set off on stage for my big moment. I was scared but ready.

I got out there, and the crowd were lovely. I sang my song. I gave it everything I possibly could. I danced, I shimmied, and I belted the song out whilst my printed-t-shirt-clad family and friends waited excitedly in the family screening area.

I got to the end of my song.

No celeb coach had turned around.

I was devastated.

It was, however, in this very moment... the moment where I thought all my dreams were shattered, that I became privy to some of the most precious advice I have ever received.

This was the year of Ricky Wilson, Rita Ora, Tom Jones and Will.I.Am.

Each of the coaches took turns to explain why they were unable to turn around for me and give me some feedback (it was all positive, btw, it turned out they had filled all their spaces, but that's showbiz, Kid) whilst I stood there stoically snot crying at them.

Will.I.Am (I'm shamelessly name-dropping here but, c'mon, this is my moment!) asked me why I was crying.

I was like, 'Will, this was my one shot. I have worked my whole life up to singing here for you guys today. I'm sad and deflated and feel like I've done myself a disservice. I could have done and been so much better...'

'Stop,' he said. 'Just stop. Breathe and listen. Gurl, you can SING. You are obviously talented. If you think that just because four people didn't say yes to you today that no-one in the world ever will? If that's what you think then you should stop now, but know this... if you are thinking 'who are you?' to carry on sharing your gift, I challenge you and say who are you NOT to?? There are 7.5 billion people in the world, and you will only be doing yourself a disservice if you stop. You have a gift, and what is a gift if you don't share it?'

In the moment, sure, it was a bitter pill to swallow. That said, the more I thought about it, the more I saw the sense in what he was saying. I gathered myself together, put my big girl pants on and decided that I would continue singing.

I have gone on to maintain my singing career and business as my sole source of income for years. I manage a full diary and have worked all over the world. My life is richer and freer for having continued despite the fact that, in that moment, I could have thrown in the towel thinking I shouldn't share my gift.

It is with this in mind that I challenge YOU, my darling reader.

Your story, your message, is your gift. Who are *you* NOT to share it? Imagine how many people are going un-helped by you, right now, because you are hiding and you don't think yourself to be important enough.

As an aside, it is worth acknowledging that, whether we like it or not, the business space is still, despite ongoing conversations, a white, CIS male-dominated environment. (Sorry, not sorry, fellas.)

We NEED you to be showing up and lighting the way for our younger generations of business owners.

We NEED to see people of colour, women, people with disabilities, members of the LGBTQ+ community and more. We all have valid and incredible stories to tell.

Our voices are important, and the more of us taking up space, the better.

Who are you NOT to speak?!

We need YOU.

OVERNIGHT SUCCESSES

It still makes me chuckle when people say that the whole, I Am The Queen Bee thing came from nowhere. Like, they woke up one morning and all of a sudden, I'm all up in their newsfeeds and networks, farting glitter and turning over six figures in my sleep.

I do not call twenty years honing my craft and failing on about a million different levels any kind of overnight success.

When you do finally get your shit together, get all of your ducks in a row and start showing up with intent and credibility, magic does begin to happen.

I want to explore with you what success actually means and if, indeed, you can create it overnight.

Success, in all of its guises, is best described using the metaphor of an iceberg.

As the tragic souls aboard the ship 'Titanic' found out in 1912, icebergs are not just formed of what you can see above the waterline. They often go way down under the water. Icebergs are much larger structures than we initially perceive.

Such is life and such is business.

Creating success takes a lot more than simply being in receipt of the spoils and trappings that come with it.

The parts that no-one wants to speak about or acknowledge are all the things you need to do and, in many instances, completely bugger up in the background, to make that success happen.

The following graphic shows what I mean:

SUCCESS.

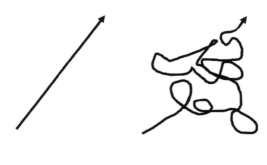

**WHAT PEOPLE THINK
IT LOOKS LIKE.**   **REALITY.**

Let's look more closely at success because if you're chasing something, you gotta know what that thing is.

Canadian leadership expert and author, Robin Sharma, best known for his best-selling book 'The Monk Who Sold His Ferrari', shares that there are eight kinds of success.

Financial/Economic Success – Money makes the world go around and is, for most, the first thing we think about when looking at success. Money makes it easier to create the life you desire and have the things you want.

The interesting thing about money is that it is an amplifier of who we truly are.

Our relationship with money will dictate how much of it we make and how much of it we keep.

Maintaining that relationship and keeping it as healthy as possible is just as important as making the stuff.

Physical Success – As we talked about in the Self-Care chapter, taking care of your body and enabling it to perform at its optimum capabilities will help you have the confidence and the energy to create even more abundance and success.

This is not to say that you need to have a number on the weighing scale in mind in order to achieve success in this area.

Seeking to feel good and have lots of energy is the one here!

Family Success – Having a happy and harmonious home life is proven to have a direct impact on how you perform in work. Making time for family, or if you have no family, other loved ones makes all of the hard work you do worthwhile.

What good is success if you have no one to share it with?

Community Success – Having that network of friends, mentors, and community helps keep your thinking fresh and your actions forward-moving. It takes a village to raise a business, not just a child.

A successful network of epic humans around you will help you feel strong and safe and ready to take the world.

Career Success – Satisfaction in the work that you do is a huge confidence builder. Having a successful career, seeing as though it's where you spend a third of your whole life, is where many of us find validation.

Doing your work and doing it well, especially if the work you do is your calling, is one of the best feelings.

Inner Success – The understanding and connection to yourself is another key to unlocking success in many of the other areas of your life. Knowing what you truly want and need, then being able to express it, is a sure-fire way of boosting the speed and level of your success.

Knowing how to navigate and manage your mindset, self-belief and inner connection are all FTW[1] here.

Adventure Success – This sounds like a level-up or an achievement unlocked in a game, and I guess it is, in many ways.

Whilst travel may not be up there on everyone's measure of success, what this represents is the requirement that all of us have, to some extent, of challenge and change.

The success here could be drawn from overcoming adversities or solving problems. It is about acknowledging our human requirement of uncertainty and exploration, just as much as we need safety and stability.

Impact Success – Contribution or giving back is a need that many humans have. This is about us having the capability and capacity to build or be part of something bigger than ourselves and seizing the opportunity to leave the world a little better than when we found it.

I'll have some of that, please.

It is not for me to tell you what your measures of success should be. It is different for everyone.

The secret sauce to most overnight successes is that the people going for it are HUNGRY.

They have their destination in mind with such clarity and purpose that they cannot help but be driven toward it.

Author and speaker, Les Brown has a famous talk about how being hungry led him from being a radio station errand boy to turn-table legend and more. It is a genuinely magnificent talk and one I regularly listen to when I need to give myself a kick up the ass.

I will pop a link to it at the back of the book so you can all experience this magical talk. There is no justice I can do it here, you need to go check it out.

For me, once the penny dropped and I knew IATQB was going to be a whole thing, I mapped out what areas were going to be my success measures and, y'all, I started running like Forrest Chuffing Gump.

BUT there have been MANY bumps in the road.

I have failed in **all** of these areas magnificently and multiple times.

I lost the house and my job.

I stopped travelling or doing anything creative for years.

I pushed everyone around me away from me because I felt like it would be better for them not to have me around.

I couldn't keep my family together, and I worry, even to this day that I have damaged my kids in ways that I can't fix and will only manifest themselves when they are older.

I got really unhealthy, I would drink too much, and I gained an unhealthy amount of weight.

I had to sacrifice time with family and friends.

I had to invest in myself over enjoying myself—a lot.

My mental health took a severe beating and remains something I have to keep a close eye on.

I would sing my shoulda-coulda-wouldas to old people in social clubs who would be impatiently waiting for me to stop singing so the bingo could begin.

I hauled my cookies up and down the country for pennies trying to make ends meet.

I went to networking meeting after networking meeting trying to be memorable.

So many times, I flailed around in the wind, praying that my sail would catch onto a breeze that would take me to dry land.

So many times, I waited for a cavalry that never arrived.

The thing is, it was all necessary because all paths have led me here, to you.

Success takes a whole heap of courage, and as Winston Churchill said,

66 **'Courage is going from failure to failure without losing enthusiasm.'**

Being super connected to what and why you're doing what you're doing and setting up those rewards along the way as we talked about previously, will help you maintain that enthusiasm so you can keep pushing forward.

Knowing this will also help you get to grips with the fact that the journey is just as important. If not more so.

I want to let you in on a little-known secret… no one really 'arrives' at success in the same way no one stays at the top of Mount Everest. Your measures of success will grow with you.

That is why it is so crucial to keep checking in with yourself and testing how you're feeling about how things are going.

Knowing that you're going to fail on the journey to success is imperative. It will allow you to move through any stumbling blocks, safe in the knowledge that it is all a natural part of the process.

Success takes hard work, persistence, rejections, risk-taking, doubts, discipline and sacrifice.

You're either learning, or you're winning. You only fail when you quit.

We can have as much success as we damn well want. We just need to *choose* to go out and get it.

Just know that it's ok if it doesn't happen overnight.

You have my permission to call bullshit on anyone who tells you otherwise.

Reflect on what YOUR measures of success are and then, if you haven't already, set some goals around them—specific

AF goals. Once you have that, you can work backwards from there. Use the 3 Stage Super Awesome Success Cycle over in Chapter 9 to help you!

---

1. FTW – For The Win, I'm down with the kids, y'all.

LOCKDOWN

I'm a bit of a knob when it comes to goals.

I am definitely not your average bear given the scrapes I get into and the speed at which I move and create these days. This mostly comes down to the fact that I am running at lightning speed away from my past and also trying to build my girls a more secure future.

I wasted a lot of time being sad and feeling sorry for myself, that I feel like sometimes it's like I'm making up for lost time.

If the year 2019 was going to be #YearOfTheQueenBee, then 2020 was going to be the #RiseOfTheHive (I do love a hashtag).

I set myself ludicrous goals to prove to myself that I'm not who I thought I was ten years ago when I believed that I was a failure and had completely stopped trusting myself.

These ridiculous goals are a reminder to myself that I'm capable of more.

They are bold declarations of trust that I can do the previously unthinkable stuff. The kind of stuff people 'like me' don't normally do.

Sometimes they feel too big.

Sometimes I get in the middle of it all and wonder what the fuck I'm doing.

Right now, for example, I have set myself the task of writing this book in two weeks. (I told you that I'm a knob.)

I wonder if it's all going to be worth it, and sometimes, I get tired and overwhelmed.

But I hadn't come this far to only come this far.

With no idea how or what it would look like, I knew that I couldn't sing five or six gigs per weekend at the same time as growing my other business. I wanted out, and I wanted IATQB to become the huge, impactful business I knew it could be. At the very least, if I was going to sing at all, I wanted to do it on my terms.

After I completed my first launch and series of IATQB events, I was finding that the potential I could both see and feel within myself and business was starting to reap real outcomes.

People all over the world, from multi-millionaire business owners and celebrities to new starters and smaller companies, were getting in touch with me to help them speak so that they could grow their brands.

I was being asked to speak on big international stages for global brands and communities.

It was a glorious, frenetic whirlwind and a testament to what happens when you do all of the things that I have shared with you in this book.

I indeed was choosing to Fly Anyway.

By February 2020 it was clear that IATQB was not going away and was going to continue to make waves and I was planning accordingly. Your girl was planning world domination.

Then the Covid 19 global pandemic hit.

WTF?!

Suddenly, it felt like the world was falling to shit, and the fear that I felt from both those around me and also rising within me felt like a boa constrictor tightening around my chest.

The media were having a field day, and the public behaved like it was an apocalypse. I am 100% sure that shares in toilet paper and pasta have never been as high as they were in March/April that year.

The first whispers of a lockdown had begun, and it was like living in a pressure cooker. We were thrown into a completely unprecedented world.

All of a sudden, we were faced with the prospect of not being able to see our loved ones or go to our places of work or education, and we had no idea when normality would return.

It was frightening and confusing for the whole world, and I hope never to experience anything like that again.

In the week that lockdown was declared, I was having a conversation with my incredible PR team, and we talked about what we could do to cheer people up. Lord knows we needed it!

I'm known in my circle for having a penchant for the ridiculous and they suggested that I do a Facebook Live stream performance whereby I would take requests and sing for the people now facing being stuck indoors for the foreseeable future.

It would be called DANIOKE!

HA!

Of course, I jumped to it and rallied my community while my press team started telling anyone who would listen that I was going to be doing an online 'happening' that coming Friday.

We set up my singing gear, naff disco lights and webcam in the front room of our tiny house and I sang song after song in both a celebration of joining together mixed with the bitter-sweetness of not knowing when the next time I would get to perform or see my family and friends in real life again was.

The Livestream ended up reaching over 36,000 people who sang and danced along in their living rooms and, just for an evening, we allowed ourselves to forget the craziness that was unfolding before us all.

This was the beginning of what was to be a rollercoaster six months for the world and for our family.

Fear is a funny beast, and I could see, hear and feel those around me getting more and more anxious about their livelihoods and their businesses.

In the aftermath of the lockdown announcements, I made a decision that I was not going to go into the situation with fear. I had survived my whole life so far, and I was ok.

The most galvanising thing for those that have lost everything is that they know what it is like to have nothing to lose. I had lost everything before, and I had survived, so nothing scared me by this point.

Knowing myself as I do, the sticky part of having to stay indoors would be maintaining a routine. It would be easy for the lie-ins to get longer and for the direction in which I was moving to become out of focus. It was with this in mind that I made sure I gave myself a reason to get up in the morning so that I could carry on building the business and not get lazy or, indeed, broke.

You may remember me telling you about when I initially began building my audience several years prior to this by going live in my car and putting my makeup on whilst musing on what was happening in the world.

There was no point re-inventing the wheel so I decided that I would make myself accountable by going live every weekday morning at 8 am to make sure I got ready for the day.

The Show Up, Wise Up, Rise Up Show was born.

After a week, I realised that it was going to get very dull, very quickly, if I was just going to talk nonsense to folk while putting my face on five times a week.

I developed a loose format, employed some snazzy software and started to interview people from the IATQB Community about what their businesses were, how they came to work in that field and how they were finding lockdown.

We have had coaches, mindset experts, health expert, advocates, teachers, and a whole spectrum of fabulous and wonderful humans join me.

I figured that if I could provide a platform for as many people as possible to share their stories and what they do, and in doing that help people that watched who may be afraid to feel more connected and less alone, it was a double win.

My fake Facebook telly show draws in hundreds of viewers every day and has become a mainstay in my day-to-day business.

When people are fearful, they often go to ground, and I was adamant that I wanted to share with those around me that they do not need to hide and that we are stronger together.

It has been wonderful seeing so many members of the IATQB Community show up, wise up and rise up together. We celebrate our successes and lift each other up through our challenges, and it is sodding glorious.

Because I remained consistent, humble, and helpful when I launched the various things that I did during this time, such as my speaking course and 1-2-1 propositions to help people get speaking, particularly online, they sold out in days.

I made sure the propositions I brought out for my audience were the things they needed and kept the delivering of real solutions to their problems right at the front of my mind.

Remember, if you have a banging strategy, great propositions, and if you come from a place of servitude, there is no reason for you not to do well, even in hard times.

In fact, I did so well that it felt a bit icky and irresponsible of me not to give back where I was able. There were people out there still fearful, and I knew there was more that I could do.

In Chapter 3, I told you about some of the fascinating things that bees do, 'festooning' being one of them.

When building new sections in their hives, honeybees link arms to help show the other bees where to build. I find this idea both endearing and powerful, and this theory forms a large part of the foundational values on which the IATQB Movement is built.

At the beginning of the 2020 lockdown, my heart sank for many reasons, one being that I knew, only too well, how it could and would be for people who were experiencing domestic abuse and domestic violence. This was an issue that I, personally, no longer had to deal with, but the thought of what I knew would be happening out there in this new locked-down environment made me sick to my stomach.

By week seven of lockdown, statistics showed that reports of domestic abuse had risen by 700%. This was a statistic that kept me awake at night.

In a non-lockdown world, domestic violence and domestic abuse occurs in 1 in 4 women and 1 in 6 men, not to mention occurrences across the gender and relationship types too. That statistic, in itself, is shocking, so to know that the number and also the degree of abuse people were experiencing as a direct result of lockdown had me shook.

As I continued going about my business, it became too uncomfortable for me to sit on this thought any longer. I needed to do something.

The Show Up Wise Up Rise Up Show had really begun to take off, and I figured that there was definitely some sort of fundraising event we could do in that format, given I had a relatively captive audience.

The Big Festoon was to be a twelve-hour extension of my morning show whereby I would interview twelve global entrepreneurs and twelve celebrities, and people would be invited to sponsor and donate to domestic abuse charities Women's Aid and Galop, the LGBTQ+ charity. A celebrity charity chat-a-thon, so to speak.

I thought that if I could both entertain, inspire and educate my entrepreneurial audience during this difficult economic period and help people experiencing domestic abuse at the same time, then it would be a win-win situation for everyone.

Creating this event was going to take some doing. I'm pretty well connected but convincing well-known TV personalities, athletes and multi-millionaires to come chat to me was going to require a little more in the way of tenacity. I needed to look at ways to stand out to and appeal to the people that I was approaching.

Even at the level at which I work, I get asked to do things all the time. There are so many charitable causes out there, that I could quite easily fill my diary up with free gigs and coaching, and this does not make for a sustainable business.

Having worked with many people in the public eye, I know that requests to do charitable work are as frequent as they are varied and, just like me in my little corner of the world, diaries and associations need to be carefully managed to keep people safe and brands congruent.

I had created a list of people who I would love to interview, entrepreneurs whose work I admired, TV personalities whose work spoke to the cause and athletes with inspirational stories.

I remember telling Wallace what I was going to do and who I wanted to participate, and he laughed. Nothing surprises him any more, bless him. He, as he always does, rolled his sleeves up and asked me what I needed.

To pull this off, I was going to have to draw on everything I knew about standing out and showing up.

We created 56 personalised videos for each of the people on my list, sharing the cause and what we would need from them. We researched their socials and best contact points, and we began sending our videos to them, praying we would get a bite.

What happened next was nothing short of a miracle.

Top TV doctor Dr Ranj, BBC's Alix Fox, multi-Olympian Tessa Sanderson CBE, Kate Hardcastle MBE, Jenny Powell and many more all got back to me to say that they would love to be involved.

People whose work I respected and admired such as Emma Sayle, Dan Meredith and Emma Kenny all said they were in without batting an eyelid.

These people did not know who I was. They didn't realise that the woman getting all up in their inbox was some scallywag chancer from the council estates in the north of England who less than a decade ago was homeless.

Each one of them accepted and believed in me and the cause, and it was because I believed in myself. I KNEW that this was something I had to do and when they saw that, they wanted to help.

Just like bees when they are flying around with their positively charged wings attracting epic flowers, I managed to gather 25 (yes, we had extra!) phenomenal humans, to interview for The Big Festoon.

From my bedroom in our tiny house in Preston, in little over three weeks, The Big Festoon was a raging success. The event reached over a million people, and we raised thousands for our chosen charities.

All this to say, my amazing friends, is that YOU are capable of incredible things, wherever you are in your journey.

As I've said before, I have lost everything in a recession, and I have had success beyond my wildest dreams during a subsequent recession. The difference was the work I had done on myself in the meantime.

I did not achieve all of these incredible things during the Covid 19 Pandemic of 2020 because I got lucky.

It was because when everyone else hid, I decided to show up.

That is what I want from each of you.

I want you to Show Up. To Wise Up. To Rise Up.

LIGHTING THE TOUCH PAPER

FOR YEARS I waited for permission to do the great things that I really wanted while other people decided they didn't want to wait and took it for themselves.

I felt like the truly good stuff just was not for me, and no one around me saw what I was capable of, so I waited and did nothing.

People like me didn't get nice houses or cars or go on holidays or help people or raise money for charity, remember.

I went around seeking external validation when, for want of a phrase less wanky, I had the power within myself all along.

I didn't realise all these things, success, abundance, health, wealth and happiness were all my birthright just as they are yours, just as they are for our very own Queen here in the UK.

True, we have to look harder for it, but it really is all there for the taking.

As it turns out, people like me CAN, people like me DO, and the glorious reality is that you can too!

We just have to be prepared to do the things that most people don't allow themselves the stamina or the permission to do.

Another quote by Jim Rohn goes:

> **"If you are not willing to risk the unusual, you will have to settle for the ordinary."**
>
> **— JIM ROHN**

We have to stop waiting for our time and sodding well take it.

My mentors and my tribe of glorious QBs helped me light the touch paper so that I could become the firecracker that you see today, but it was all already there, I just needed to remember who the eff I was.

It is coming to the end of our time together in this book and I hope it has given you some ideas as to how you can really step up into *your* birthright of all the awesome stuff.

If this is the permission *you* need to go out there and build the life you actually want instead of playing small and safe, I hereby grant you all of it!

Stop dicking around, put your crown on, get that good shit and revel in your awesomeness!

I want to hear all about the epic stuff you create.

You are The Queen[1] Bee after all!

Hugest love,

Dani xx

---

1. Also King Bees and Royal Bees... I SEE YOU... I needed a snappy way to close out!

HELPING OTHERS TO FLY ANYWAY

It was always my intention, from the second I heard the Bee Movie quote about bees caring not what humans think is impossible, to create a foundation that would help survivors of domestic abuse build businesses so that they could do just that, Fly Anyway.

Taking back control of your life after you have escaped a toxic relationship is incredibly difficult. Learning to trust yourself, your talents and believing in your worth as an independent, whole person is a constant struggle, especially if you are trying to do that on your own.

The Fly Anyway Foundation was launched in 2020 to help survivors access some of the best business mentors and business service providers in the UK and eventually globally, to help them to build successful and sustainable businesses.

You can find out more about our work, how you can become an ambassador or how else you can support at: www.iamthequeenbee.co.uk/flyanyway

All profits from the IATQB merchandise line goes to the Fly Anyway Foundation; you can check out our shop here:

www.iamthequeenbee.co.uk/shop

ACKNOWLEDGMENTS

As an avid reader when I was growing up, I would always read the acknowledgements at the back of the book.

I would find it fascinating that there were so many people to thank and wondered if I ever got to writing a proper book, would I have so many people to thank?

Turns out writing a book is a journey in its own right and yes, there are a butt tonne of people I need to thank!

First of all, to my gorgeous friend, soul sister and publisher, Abigail Horne. Your mission to help people share their stories is just phenomenal. You are changing the world, one book at a time and I am proud to work with you. Thank you for your unwavering belief in me and my abilities. You have my heart.

Jo Swan and the team at Chocolate PR, from the first time we spoke to every idea we have cooked up since, it is a joy to work with you and have you on TEAM QB. We're only just getting started.

Every book needs a midwife, and Danielle Hansen, my amazing Operations Manager, you have mopped my brow and held my hand from conception to contractions, transition to pushing. Thank you for being with me every step of the way and believing I can, even when I didn't. I'm so excited for our continued adventures.

To my assistant Anna Foxx, you have shown awe-inspiring strength whilst I have been beavering away on this book. Your support is valued, and you are so loved.

My beta readers, what a team of luscious wonder-humans, in particular, Nat Walker, whose advice, love and Isla baby spam has been invaluable.

To Ami Matona for creating the most beautiful Queen Bee gown. Your work is world class and it's an honour to rock the masterpiece that you made.

My mentors, all of you, for being who I needed when I needed it. Having people like you who are blazing a trail for people like me helps us see what possible.

My business sisters, my safe people and my line-backers Nicki James, Deep Bajwa and Sam Bearfoot. When no one else understands the late nights, the sacrifice and the grind, you do. More champagne meetups, please, we have much to celebrate.

My amazing family, for holding the fort while I build our legacy. Let's keep breaking the cycles and coming back stronger.

Wallace, for never holding me back. For opening up the cage that I was in and allowing me to fly anyway. Your strength and support, even when I tell you about my next batshit idea, never ceases to amaze me. You are the King to my Queen.

My Flowers, all this for you. You have shown such incredible strength and understanding while Mummy is building our castle. We have so much to look forward to, my loves.

Finally, to my QBs, your unwavering belief in the IATQB Movement and in me has my heart full. We are changing the world, and I am proud to festoon with you. You inspire me every second of every day. Look at all the things we are creating together.

USEFUL LINKS AND HELPFUL STUFF

I have mentioned, at various points in the book, that I would pop some helpful links here at the back for you.

Mental Health

MIND www.mind.org.uk Tel: 0300 123 3393

Samaritans www.samaritans.org – Tel: 116 123

CALM www.thecalmzone.net Tel: 0800 58 58 58

Domestic Abuse

National Domestic Abuse Helpline

www.nationaldahelpline.org.uk Tel: 0808 2000 247

Women's Aid www.womensaid.org.uk

Galop (LGBTQ+) www.galop.org.uk Tel: 0800 999 5428

Les Brown 'Hungry' Talk

https://www.youtube.com/watch?v=SDIE_QPOPzo

WERK WITH DANI!

You can get involved with the IATQB Movement by joining the IATQB Hive on Facebook:

www.facebook.com/groups/TheIATQBHive

You can find out about how to book Dani to speak for your organisation by emailing:

bookings@iamthequeenbee.co.uk

All details of Dani's courses, future events and how you can work with her 1-2-1 can be found at:

www.iamthequeenbee.co.uk

BEE HEARD - So You Wanna Be A Speaker Waitlist

https://thequeenbeedani.kartra.com/page/beeheardwaitlist

Here are some links to some masterclasses that I have created for you that you may find helpful:

Mega Helpful Tips For Speaking

https://thequeenbeedani.kartra.com/
page/speakingmasterclass

Show Up, Wise Up, Rise Up Masterclass

https://thequeenbeedani.kartra.com/
page/suwurumasterclass